A Bad Day At Gopher's Breath

A Farce In Thirteen Scenes

by
Al Ver Schure
and Lee Ver Schure

A SAMUEL FRENCH ACTING EDITION

New York Hollywood London Toronto
SAMUELFRENCH.COM

Copyright © 1975 by Al Ver Schure and Lee Ver Schure

ALL RIGHTS RESERVED

CAUTION: Professionals and amateurs are hereby warned that *A BAD DAY AT GOPHER'S BREATH* is subject to a licensing fee. It is fully protected under the copyright laws of the United States of America, the British Commonwealth, including Canada, and all other countries of the Copyright Union. All rights, including professional, amateur, motion picture, recitation, lecturing, public reading, radio broadcasting, television and the rights of translation into foreign languages are strictly reserved. In its present form the play is dedicated to the reading public only.

The amateur live stage performance rights to *A BAD DAY AT GOPHER'S BREATH* are controlled exclusively by Samuel French, Inc., and licensing arrangements and performance licenses must be secured well in advance of presentation. PLEASE NOTE that amateur licensing fees are set upon application in accordance with your producing circumstances. When applying for a license quotation and performance license please give us the number of performances intended, dates of production, your seating capacity and admission fee. Licensing fees are payable one week before the opening performance of the play to Samuel French, Inc., at 45 W. 25th Street, New York, NY 10010.

licensing fees of the required amount must be paid whether the play is presented for charity or gain and whether or not admission is charged.

Stock licensing fee quoted upon application to Samuel French, Inc.

For all other rights than those stipulated above, apply to: Samuel French, Inc.

Particular emphasis is laid on the question of amateur or professional readings, permission and terms for which must be secured in writing from Samuel French, Inc.

Copying from this book in whole or in part is strictly forbidden by law, and the right of performance is not transferable.

Whenever the play is produced the following notice must appear on all programs, printing and advertising for the play: "Produced by special arrangement with Samuel French, Inc."

Due authorship credit must be given on all programs, printing and advertising for the play.

No one shall commit or authorize any act or omission by which the copyright of, or the right to copyright, this play may be impaired.
No one shall make any changes in this play for the purpose of production.
Publication of this play does not imply availability for performance. Both amateurs and professionals considering a production are strongly advised in their own interests to apply to Samuel French, Inc., for written permission before starting rehearsals, advertising, or booking a theatre.
No part of this book may be reproduced, stored in a retrieval system, or transmitted in any form, by any means, now known or yet to be invented, including mechanical, electronic, photocopying, recording, videotaping, or otherwise, without the prior written permission of the publisher.

ISBN 978-0-573-62061-4   Printed in U.S.A.   **#250**

DESCRIPTION OF THE PLAY

Coming off a trail of failures, ineptitude, stupidity, and dirt, the notorious Rawlins gang rides into Gopher's Breath to pull off one last bank robbery, and steal the gold in the famous Clutzmeyer Safe. While Rawhide Rawlins wants to fulfill the dream of a potato farm in Idaho for Mom Rawlins, Sheriff Amos Crutchwaffle—representing all that's rotten in Gopher's Breath—also has his designs on the loot. With his past hot on his heels, Crutchwaffle needs the payroll to escape the clutches of Fat Jack Caldwell, the most feared man in the West. Both outlaw and sheriff find their plans altered by the presence of each other and that of the banker's niece, the beautiful Bambi Phingerdoo.

Stricken by love, a reformed Rawhide tries desperately to go straight; driven by hunger, his gang carries on in spite of him; and, consumed by greed and fear, Crutchwaffle manipulates the rest to his own evil ends. Predictably, love deals Crutchwaffle a bad draw in the end, and Bambi and Rawhide ride happily into the sunset.

Riddled with all the time-worn, traditional cliches that constitute a comical overkill of the classic western, Gopher's Breath becomes the setting for bungled bank robberies, temperance demonstrations, shoot-outs, showdowns, true love, and the wrath of a woman scorned. Leaving no stone unturned, "A Bad Day at Gopher's Breath" is a western that goes one step beyond having something for everyone.

A BAD DAY AT GOPHER'S BREATH was first presented at Hamilton Community High School, in Hamilton, Michigan, on November 14, 1972. It was directed by Al Ver Schure. The cast of characters was as follows:

AMOS CRUTCHWAFFLE ....*Jim Kleinheksel*
    the sheriff of Gopher's Breath and second most feared man in the West

BELLE DURHAM ....*Kathi Wolters*
    the saloon proprietress and Amos' companion

RALPH "RAWHIDE" RAWLINS ....*John Wilson*
    the notorious gang leader

BAMBI PHINGERDOO ....*Beth Wolters*
    the banker's niece

PANDORA CRUTCHWAFFLE ....*Lynda Folkert*
    Amos' elder spinster sister and leading temperance advocate

FAT JACK CALDWELL ....*Paul Zuverink*
    bounty hunter and most feared man in the West

THE NARRATOR ....*Bill Goen*

THE RAWLINS GANG:

BAD BRUCE ....*Bob Busscher*
RINGO ....*Jim Kaniff*
LAREDO ....*Tom Schaap*
DOC ....*Gregg Deters*
SLEEPY ....*Tim Kleinheksel*
DOPEY ....*Tom Rigterink*

AND:

BARKEEP ....*Lee Becksfort*
PIANO-PLAYER ....*Judy Schaap*
BANK TELLER ....*Karl Meyer*
THE INDIAN, RABBIT EARS ....*Joe Boeve*
GENERAL CUSTER ....*Larry Custer*
COWBOYS ....*Dave VerHoeven, Tom Boerigter,
    Lynn Van Order, Kraig Meyer,* and *Terry Schipper*
SALOON GIRLS, APRIL, MAY, and JUNE ....*Jane Naber,
    Stephanie Topp,* and *Cindi Bledsoe*
TEMPERANCE LADIES ..*Brenda Ellens, Marcia Myaard,
    Kris Barkel, Joyce Immink,* and *Phyllis Stehower*

A Bad Day at Gopher's Breath

SCENE 1

The Curtain is opened as house lights fade and remains open throughout the play. Recorded selections of old western favorites, which may have been playing now fade out as the NARRATOR [who must also play guitar] takes a seat on the Down Right edge of the Stage in the light of a single spot, and the PIANO-PLAYER is seated at the piano. Together, they play a number or two, and then the music fades.

NARRATOR: Howdy. Reckon it was about 1842, when a feller, name of Morris Plasman, left Illinois in search of the precious metal, gold. Round 1852, he landed in the Cherry Creek goldfields—now called Denver—and havin' just missed the strike there, gave up on gold and headed southwest, havin' acquired through five-card stud (and an extra card, I hear) what was reputed to be a genuine map of the fabled Lost Chinchilla mine of the Hopi's. He crossed Bald Mountain and Boreas Pass, and somewhere between Fair Play and Leadville, Morris gave up on the Chinchilla dream too, and instead founded the town of Gopher's Breath, Colorado Territory. (*Here, the NARRATOR begins playing the theme, "A Bad Day in Gopher's Breath," and sings:*)

8 A BAD DAY AT GOPHER'S BREATH
Title Theme
"A BAD DAY IN GOPHER'S BREATH"
by Lee Ver Schure

"Now listen here, stranger; I'll sing you a song
'Bout a town in the wild, rugged West—
Where a six-gun's the judge
And a bullet's the jury,
In the town that they call Gopher's Breath.

You may be a good man, you may be a bad man—
In Gopher's Breath, it's all the same.
For, if you cross the sheriff,
As sure as the sunset,
There's a bullet a wearin' your name.

Monday through Sunday—now each day's the same;
Burning sun, choking dust and quick death.
There's no day's a good day—
You'll be sorry you came—
Every day's a bad day in Gopher's Breath . . .
Any day's a bad day in Gopher's Breath . . .
Today's a bad day in Gopher's Breath . . ."

(*The music for the theme is a variation of the traditional "Streets of Laredo." At the conclusion of the song, the guitarist and pianist continue playing as the lights come up on the saloon, and when full lighting is achieved, the piano begins to bang out saloon-type honky-tonk.* BELLE *is at the Upstage end of the bar with the* BARKEEP; *two cowboys are at the Down Left table playing cards. The girls are scattered about.* RABBIT EARS *is slumped over the Upstage table. A cowboy enters and walks to the bar.*)

A BAD DAY AT GOPHER'S BREATH 9

BARKEEP. What'll it be, stranger?
FIRST COWBOY. Gimme a shot of rotgut, Barkeep.
(*As the* FIRST COWBOY *is being cared for, an obviously young man enters and walks timidly to the bar.*)
BARKEEP. What'll it be, stranger?
SECOND COWBOY. (*In a squeaky voice.*) I'll have a sarsaparilla, Mister.

(*The music cuts off abruptly on a sour note as Sheriff* AMOS CRUTCHWAFFLE *strides through the swinging doors in a grandiose entrance. He waits, expecting some response. The Sheriff is an aging gunfighter, graying around the temples, reputed to be the second fastest gun in the West. He is lean, mean, scarred, and wears a patch over his left eye, his hair long and greased back. He wears a black frock coat, vest, string tie, jangling spurs, and two guns slung low. Getting little attention, he checks his watch and leans forward in a half crouch.*)

AMOS. (*To the young man.*) All right, cowpoke! (*He pauses.*) I reckon you must be tarred o' livin'. (*Everyone in the bar has now taken notice and moved out of the line of fire except the* SECOND COWBOY.) Turn around, hombre! (*There is surprised recognition.*) Yeah, you, I say; are you not the bushwhackin' rascal, Tom Dawes?? Well?
SECOND COWBOY. (*Thunderstruck.*) Yeah, uh, sure, I'm . . . not . . .
THIRD COWBOY. (*At the table.*) No, Sheriff, you got no truck with him. I reckon . . .
AMOS. (*Wheeling on him.*) Who asked you to come a jawin' into this? You jest rest easy lessin' you want to cut into this affair. Now, (*Turning back to* SECOND COWBOY.) you, you jest punched yer last cow, broke yer last pony, downed yer last rotgut . . . uh, . . . uh, . . . carved yer last notch, stole yer last kiss . . .!!
SECOND COWBOY. (*In panic.*) Sheriff, what did I do?

10 A BAD DAY AT GOPHER'S BREATH

Amos. I'll tell ya, ya lawless sidewinder; you cashed in yer chips . . .

Second Cowboy. No, no! I'm only fourteen and on an errand for my . . .

Amos. Don't interrupt me! Ya got along yer last little dogie, ya . . . uh, . . . uh, . . . ah . . .

Second Cowboy. Sheriff!!

Amos. (*Yelling.*) Don't go a tryin' to change ponies in the middle of the Pecos . . . (*He draws and fires three or four times. The cowboy falls.*) Sonny . . . (*He pauses.*) Hell, he shouldn't a gone an' riled me. (*He blows on his smoking gun barrels, twirls them and puts them back in his holsters.*)

Belle. (*She is an aging saloon queen, a few years younger than* Amos, *for whom she has always been a ready companion. She has a hard but striking beauty, due partly, perhaps, to her attire and her quality of being the proprietress of the establishment.* Belle *wears a velvet, floor-length gown, long dark, flowing hair, and an overabundance of jewelry. She portrays an unrequited love.*) What did the poor skunk do, Amos?

Amos. (*He leans against the bar.*) Belle, you *know* I run a tight town. That there varmint missed his curfew, missed his stage . . . Why, (*He laughs.*) I'm plumb surprised he even hit the floor.

Belle. That's not the cowboy you told to be out of town on the 5:00 stage, Amos.

Amos. No?

Belle. No. (*A cowboy leaves the table, headed for the door.*) I reckon it be the one what's headed for the door there.

Amos. Yer right as rain, Belle. And I aim to make up fer my mistake. (*He steps over the body, strides to the door, aims carefully, and fires one shot into the street. A scream is heard in the distance.*) There. Saved myself some lead on that one—I always average somewheres around four slugs per criminal.

A BAD DAY AT GOPHER'S BREATH 11

BELLE. That there second one—out there ... weren't no criminal either, Amos; leastways not yet. Tain't 5:00 yet. The stage is still due ... You haven't forgot the payroll comin' in for the Phingerdoo bank?

AMOS. Ah, yes. Indeed I have not. That fortune has my—or should I say "our"—undivided attention. (*He stops, lost in reflection.*) And as for those two (*Points to bodies.*) I always say, "Nothing ventured; nothing gained." (*He flips a coin to Barkeep.*) Here, Barkeep. Plug the holes I made. (*Turns to leave.*) I like to run a tight town.

SCENE 2

The setting changes to the interior of the hideout. "RAWHIDE" RAWLINS is pacing Upstage of the table area. DOC is cleaning his rifle on the Upstage cot; LAREDO is lying on the Downstage cot. BAD BRUCE sits at one end of the table, SLEEPY, DOPEY, and RINGO together on the other end. BRUCE jealously guards a couple of cans of beans; the three opposite him are fighting frantically for a remaining can.

RAWHIDE. (*Screaming.*) For the last time, it's Gopher's Breath! I don't want to talk about it anymore!

LAREDO. Ya must of lost yer horsesense, Rawhide. It's plumb loco to go inta Gopher's Breath. That sheriff runs a tight town. (*Pauses.*) I'm fer knockin' over Santa Fe.

DOC. I'm with Laredo. If you go to Gopher's Breath, count me out.

RINGO. Yeah!

RAWHIDE. (*Turning to him.*) Yeah, what?

RINGO. Yeah, that sheriff runs a tight town; I don't wanna die with my boots on.

12 A BAD DAY AT GOPHER'S BREATH

RAWHIDE. (*Like a maniac.*) Then you'd better pull 'em off now, ya sorry excuse— Cause I'm gonna fill ya full of holes if ya don't shut up!! (*Draws guns and pauses.*) . . . Now, shut up!! (*He tries to begin again, more calmly.*) Listen, fellas. We been together a long time now . . . We made some real loot together . . .

SLEEPY. Uh, . . . when?

RAWHIDE. Shut up! (*Hits him with his hat.*) . . . And since this is our last job, and it's for my mother, it's got to be quality . . . Quality, ya hear?

DOC. We ain't never worried about quality before.

RINGO. Yeah! (RAWHIDE *hits him with his hat— He adds quickly.*) Course we ain't ever needed it.

RAWHIDE. (*Recovering and pausing again.*) All right, all right, boys. I see we're at an impasse. (*They look around.*) So, I'll back up a ways to where we can agree. Now, I know it don't matter none to you guys if Mom gets her potato farm in Idaho, the one what she's dreamed of fer nigh to twenty years, or that she ain't et real regular since I give up store clerkin'. I know none of that concerns ya. (*He pauses again to wipe a tear from his eye; he holds his hat in front of him.* RINGO, SLEEPY, DOPEY, *and* BRUCE *all sob, wipe noses, etc.*)

DOC. (*Sarcastically.*) 'Scuse me whilst I go fetch my violin . . . (*He stands and tips his hat as if to leave.*)

BRUCE. (*Raging and wheeling on him, hand on his gun.*) I had a mother once!! . . . (*He trails off.*) 'Course she left me when I was big enough to fend fer myself. (*He turns back.*)

DOC. Just as well. She'd be one more cut in the profits of this gang if'n she'd waited till you was smart enough too. (BRUCE *flies at* DOC, *gun drawn, but* RAWHIDE *steps between and restores order.*)

RAWHIDE. Listen! Listen! What *does* matter to ya— the only thing that matters to all of us—is the Phingerdoo fortune in the famous Clutzmeyer safe . . . There's

A BAD DAY AT GOPHER'S BREATH 13

gonna be a powerful lot of cash in Gopher's Breath when that payroll comes in! (*He waits expectantly.* RINGO, SLEEPY, *and* DOPEY *get excited, rubbing hands together, etc.* BRUCE *is in deep thought.* LAREDO *is bemused;* DOC *is disgusted.* BRUCE *then raises his hand as if to offer an opinion. All are amazed.*)

BRUCE. Uh, . . . uh . . .

RAWHIDE. Yeah, Bruce? It's, uh, good to see ya gettin' involved in the plannin' . . .

BRUCE. Plannin'? What plannin'?

RAWHIDE. Well, I figgered you had something to offer er add . . .

DOC. Naw, he was just scratchin' at flies.

BRUCE. (*Flinging his chair back to confront* DOC; RAWHIDE *immediately in between.*) You sayin' them's my flies??

DOC. Well, they sure as hell ain't . . .

RAWHIDE. (*Stopping* DOC.) Doc!

DOC. (*First glares, then turns back to cleaning his rifle.*) No, sir. Sure ain't often we hear from Bruce . . . No, sir.

BRUCE. (*After a nod from* RAWHIDE.) Uh, uh . . .

RAWHIDE. Bruce? (*Most lean in eagerly to hear.*)

BRUCE. (*Surly.*) What!? (*Then childlike.*) Yeah, uh, we sure, uh, better knock over a big one, uh . . . this time.

DOC. (*Still baiting* BRUCE.) I can't imagine why.

BRUCE. (*Turns on* DOC—*the tension is heavy.* RINGO, SLEEPY, DOPEY, *and* LAREDO *all dive onto the floor, plugging their ears. Then, after a long pause,* BRUCE *backs off and continues to* RAWHIDE *with something of a higher priority than gunplay.*) Cause I calculate that, uh . . . (*He counts on his fingers.*) I'm about three, maybe four weeks behind on my allowance, Ralph . . . Ya owe me, uh, . . . about two-fifty, three dollars!! (*There is general accord from* RINGO, SLEEPY, DOPEY, *and* LAREDO.)

SLEEPY. We sure had to get a lotta allowances outa that last job, payin' so poorly as it did!

LAREDO. Never were no money in stealin' from kids.

BRUCE. (*Really into the spirit of it now.*) Ralph, you been stingy with our money!!

RINGO and DOPEY. Yeah!

SLEEPY. Yeah!

BRUCE. (*Thinking.*) Yeah!

RINGO. Yeah! (*He pokes* DOPEY *to say it again.*)

DOC. (*Quickly on his feet.*) Ah, hell, don't start *that* again! Gopher's Breath can't be no worse'n this. What do ya say, Laredo?

LAREDO. Well, mebbe yer right. That payroll surely is a temptation . . . Lord knows I crave a square meal . . . but I don't fancy no servin' of hot lead from Amos Crutchwaffle.

DOPEY. Yeah, he runs a tight town.

DOC. All right, Rawhide— You and . . . *them*, knock over the bank. Me and the "widow-maker" here— (*Pats his rifle.*) will take care of Amos Crutchwaffle.

SCENE 3

The setting is the interior of the First Phingerdoo Savings & Trust. As the lights come up, we find Miss BAMBI PHINGERDOO *behind the partition which separates the main lobby from the employees' work area. She is readying the bank for daily transactions as the door is opened by* AMOS CRUTCHWAFFLE. BAMBI *is young, beautiful, and rosy-cheeked; she is dressed in gingham, and is above all else naive and innocent.* AMOS *stalks in, spurs jingling, and plants himself near the doorway, waiting for her attention and approval . . . Upon not getting either, he begins a long grooming process. He straightens his string tie, buffs his boot-tops on the backs of his trouser legs; he ad-*

A BAD DAY AT GOPHER'S BREATH 15

justs his hat, guns, and star, twirls the ends of his mustache in a somewhat sinister manner. Unaccustomed to having to identify his presence, he now begins hoarsely and ungentlemanly clearing his throat and shifting from one foot to the other. And, finally,

BAMBI. Oh, Sheriff Crutchwaffle, you quite startled me.

AMOS. (*Stepping in.*) Miss Phingerdoo, you are ravishing in that gown.

BAMBI. Oh, this is only a uniform, fit for daily drudgery.

AMOS. (*Opening the gate in the partition to usher her through.*) And drudgery it must surely be, as your Uncle Phidias is off in St. Louis on matters of finance . . .

BAMBI. (*Interrupting, innocently.*) I know.

AMOS. I know you know . . . You need someone to help in overseeing this vast fortune—I mean, institution of trust.

BAMBI. Well, there is our faithful teller, Coggins. He has given his best years to the bank.

AMOS. More than that. But I mean someone strong, resourceful, and bold of action.

BAMBI. Oh, you are right, Sheriff . . . But who?

AMOS. Miss Phingerdoo, I . . .

BAMBI. (*Shocked.*) Not you, Sheriff Crutchwaffle!

AMOS. Why not, Miss Bambi? Surely I need not prove myself to the good citizens of Gopher's Breath. But wait—if I must prove my capabilities to you, there is . . . (*He pauses.*) a social at the church Saturday at which . . .

BAMBI. (*Interrupting again.*) Oh, I could not avail myself to you, socially, Sheriff—

AMOS. Miss Bambi?

BAMBI. I would do myself an injustice accompanying a man who . . . (*She shudders.*) lives by the gun. After all, Sheriff, this *is* the Nineteenth Century.

16   A BAD DAY AT GOPHER'S BREATH

AMOS. Ah, yes . . . These (*He draws his pistols and stares at them, becoming lost in reverie; then he twirls them around and flips them into his holsters. He pats them lovingly.*) are a necessary evil, I assure you.

BAMBI. Necessary?

AMOS. Surely a young lady as rich—er, as comely, as yourself, placed in such a high position of responsibility, is aware of the necessity of protection against the vile forces of evil . . . Miss Bambi, I implore you to think of the dangers of managing a fortune—er, ah, bank in this reckless age . . . the men of ill repute, (*He leans in menacingly, almost leering.*) scum of the earth, dregs of the barrel, the slime on the river, ah, the mold off the loaf, who have no scruples, who live constantly in the shadow of greed and lust . . .

BAMBI. Oh, Sheriff, you quite frighten me. (*She recoils from him, and he snaps out of his train of thought.*)

AMOS. Only so you will not think less of me because of my profession . . . But enough of that. Perhaps we could talk of other things, . . . over dinner at Delmonico's?

BAMBI. Oh, Sheriff Crutchwaffle, really I should not . . . (*She pauses.*) However . . .

AMOS. Fine. It is a date then; shall we say, 6:00?

BAMBI. But—

AMOS. Until then, Miss Bambi. (*He touches his hat and backs out of the door. A bit of slapstick will work well here if* AMOS *takes off his hat as he is backing out and catches the brim in the door as it closes, necessitating him to again partially open the door and whisk out his hat.*)

SCENE 4

The setting is the interior of the saloon the next day. Cowboys and saloon girls are scattered about;

A BAD DAY AT GOPHER'S BREATH 17

RABBIT EARS *is at his usual spot.* BELLE *and* AMOS *are at the Downstage Right table talking. There is honky-tonk music as the lights come up.*

BELLE. I chanced by the bank t'other night and saw ya palaverin' with that hoity-toity Bambi Phingerdoo— What in tarnation, Amos . . .? I sell the only stock you ever bought into.

AMOS. Yer eyes sparkle when yer mad, Belle. They only shine brighter through the bottom of a glass.

BELLE. You ain't playin' me false, are ya? Cause there's somethin' I can tell ya that ya oughta know . . .

AMOS. What you drivin' at, Belle . . . honey?

BELLE. If'n yer true to me, Amos, you'll answer my question first.

AMOS. Whoa, Belle. Don't git yer dander up; I'll explain it all, but first tell me whut's rotten in Gopher's Breath.

BELLE. All right. A skinner from the mule train told Barkeep he met a varmint what's lookin' fer a gunslinger with a patch over his left eye and a long scar . . . Skinner, he suspected the hombre was after a bounty. Ain't many men that match that description, Amos . . .

AMOS. 'pears my gunslingin' days in Tombstone are hot on my heels, Belle. It's bound to be Fat Jack Caldwell.

BELLE. The bounty hunter? You mean the one they call the most feared man in the West? . . . Why I heered he's so cussed mean he wears a rattlesnake fer a necktie; he sharpens his Bowie knife on his whiskers; he smokes his cee-gars backwards—why, his idea of fun is spittin' into the wind!

AMOS. Oh, pshaw! Ya cain't believe all ya hear, Belle. I know fer a fact Fat Jack Caldwell's jest a man . . . , and if'n I shoot a hole in him, he's bound to bleed.

BELLE. Then you aim to play out yer hand. It looks

stacked agin ya— He might kill ya. After all, yer only the second most feared man in the West.

AMOS. (*Nervously attempting to be light.*) How kin I lose if yer behind me, Belle. Love will spur me on; it has never failed me yet. (*He leans in.*) Mebbe we kin bushwhack him . . . ?

BELLE. Amos, you're barkin' up the wrong tree. I want you to hang up them consarn things . . . (*Points to guns.*) I don't want to help ya use 'em.

AMOS. You did one other time, Belle, honey. (*He pauses.*)

BELLE. That's only 'cause the "lady" would have killed ya. Anyhow, you don't think yer up to him?

AMOS. I never said that! (*He stands, shoving back his chair.*) We'll jes' see about it if'n he ever rides into Gopher's Breath.

BELLE. Then you mean you'll face up to him?

AMOS. If'n he gives me that chance. And that means I'll have to see him a'fore he sees me; otherwise I'll buy a bullet in the back.

BELLE. (*In real surprise.*) Imagine! As fast as all that and he's still no fairer than you are!

AMOS. (*After a long pause.*) If'n you don't want to help me shoot Fat Jack, at least keep yer eyes peeled and yer ears open— He's bound to light in here sooner er later. —And the same goes fer Barkeep and the girls too.

BELLE. Now, what of the delicate Miss Phingerdoo?

AMOS. Ah, yes. Come closer so we can talk. I suspected that my future in Gopher's Breath couldn't last forever—there's too many sidewinders like Fat Jack . . . So I been plannin' a future in Mexico, for two, Belle—just you and me.

BELLE. It's a future I ain't seen. You done a passle of talkin'—more'n most women wouldda cared to listen to—but ya can't build on hot air, Amos. How are ya gonna build our future this time?

AMOS. You kin start yer packin', Belle, honey. We're

A BAD DAY AT GOPHER'S BREATH

travelin' on the . . . (*Whispers loudly.*) Phingerdoo fortune—the gold in the Clutzmeyer safe. I'm only playin' up to Bambi Phingerdoo as part of my plan.

BELLE. Well, just remember that you're only 'spozed to be play-actin' . . . (*She pauses.*) You certain this is the best way to get that money?

AMOS. You know I cain't abide shootin' women, Belle. Once I'm in Miss Phingerdoo's favor, . . . I can use my position to gain the combination to her safe.

BELLE. But, Amos, do you think she'll fall fer that?

AMOS. Most assuredly, Belle. Though Miss Phingerdoo is as pure as mountain water, she's a drip.

SCENE 5

The interior of the gang's hideout, at about the same time. RAWHIDE *is going over the plans for the robbery of the bank for one last time. As with all the other times, hardly anyone is listening.* Doc *leans against the Upstage Right "wall,"* BRUCE *and* DOPEY *sit on the Stage Left cot;* SLEEPY *sits on the Upstage end of the table, with* LAREDO *and* RINGO *on the Downstage end.* DOPEY *hungrily watches* BRUCE *eat something, and the three at the table fight over a food can.* RAWHIDE *is poring over a map on the table.*

RAWHIDE. (*Over all the shouting, which subsides a bit.*) All right! All right. We're going over this plan one more time, and this is the last time . . . Right? (Doc *looks disgusted.*)

THE OTHERS. Right! and Right, Ralph!

RAWHIDE. Here it is. Everybody's gonna get it right, right?

THE GANG. Right!

RAWHIDE. Cause we all *got* to get it . . . Now, Dopey, you got the note . . .

DOPEY. Yup.
RAWHIDE. Now, fellas, like I said all the other times, you might say Dopey is the key to our success—
THE GANG. (*Interrupting.*) Dopey??
RAWHIDE. (*After a pause.*) ". . . Cause he's got the note. So once more, here's what we're gonna do: First; Dopey goes in first, followed by me; then Ringo— Doc is fourth, Sleepy, fifth, Laredo, sixth, and Bruce, yer seventh.
DOC. Bruce— Hear that? Yer last!
BRUCE. That's cuz Ralph has somethin' special fer me to do.
DOC. That's cause you'd get lost if you was first!
BRUCE. (*Turning on him for a confrontation.*) Oh, yeah?!
RAWHIDE. (*Stepping in between.*) Hold it! Hold it! (*He notices* DOPEY'S *hand up.*) Yeah, ah, Dopey? Make it quick; we got to git done.
DOPEY. I'll help find Bruce if he gits lost.
RAWHIDE. It's not in the plan, Dopey.
RINGO. We could still put it in, Rawhide . . .
RAWHIDE. (*Through clenched teeth, after a long pause; his hand on his gun.*) We gonna argue over nuthin', or we gonna go through the plan?
DOPEY. (*Enthusiastically.*) We're goin' through the plan, Ralph!
THE GANG. Right!
RAWHIDE. (*Turning and striding Upstage Left.*) O.k. Second; when Dopey is three paces from the teller, Bruce, you cover the window . . . (*He comes back to the table.*) here. Third; Sleepy and Doc— When Dopey hands the note to the teller, you fellas will be by this little fence in case the president or anyone gets wise. Be sure to be there then, . . . but not before. (*He moves back Upstage Left.*) Fourth; also when the note is handed in, Ringo, you go and sit down on the bench across from Bruce's left . . .
RINGO. (*Interrupting.*) Uh, . . . Which side will

A BAD DAY AT GOPHER'S BREATH 21

Bruce's left be on? . . . Like if he's facing the window, his left will be on a different side than if he's facing the rest of ya's . . .

RAWHIDE. (*Shouting and moving back to his map.*) Look! Look! The bench is always across from the left side of the window! O.k.? (*He pauses.*) Now, don't just come in and sit right down; it'll look funny. So, wait fer the note to be handed. (*He pauses again and moves Downstage Left.*) Fifth; when Ringo sits, I'll light up my cigar and wait in line behind Dopey. When I light up, Laredo, you move to the right of the teller and also light up. You and I will be watching the customers . . . and be sure you've got matches. Sixth; when we both light up, Bruce, you make sure the front door gets locked by the bolt that's on it.

BRUCE. (*In panic.*) I gotta watch the window *and* the door??

RAWHIDE. (*Giving* BRUCE *a dirty look.*) Seventh; After the teller reads the note and heads fer the safe . . . (*He moves back toward Upstage Left.*) Sleepy and Doc, you guys— (*Just as* RAWHIDE *passes the Upstage end of the table, heading Upstage Left,* SLEEPY *dives onto the floor in panic.*)

SLEEPY. (*Screaming.*) My bean! My bean! I dropped my bean! (SLEEPY *is on the floor, searching behind* RAWHIDE'S *back, in an instant; simultaneously,* RINGO, LAREDO, DOPEY, *and* BRUCE *join in. Their search lasts perhaps fifteen seconds when all notice above them the silent wrath of their leader. There is a tense moment; then they sheepishly climb back into their seats.*) Oh, well, I guess it don't matter none, one bean. (*Then, spotting it, while* RAWHIDE *is still staring them down.*) . . . Here it is; I found my bean!

(RINGO, LAREDO, *and* SLEEPY *then resume their fight over* SLEEPY'S *bean. Statements can be uttered as* "It's my bean," "I found it," *and* "No, it's mine." RAWHIDE *finally resumes the strategy session.*)

22 A BAD DAY AT GOPHER'S BREATH

RAWHIDE. (*Backing up a bit.*) After the teller reads the note and he heads fer the safe, Sleepy and Doc, you guys follow him— Go through the little gate . . . here. (*He pauses.*) Now, there's only five more points —everybody got their assignments so far? (THE GANG *looks really confused—muttering, conferring, pointing, counting on their fingers, etc.* Doc *looks disgusted.*) O.k., eighth; by this time, the customers will get wise, so Laredo, Ringo, and I will draw our guns and clean out the teller's cage— I'll do that— You two get valuables off the customers and help. Ninth; . . . (RINGO *and* DOPEY *alternately and sheepishly raise their hands.*) Yeah, uh, . . . Dopey?

DOPEY. Yeah, uh, . . . Do I come in, er, uh, wait out in the street?

RINGO. Yeah, Rawhide, when do I light up my cigar?

(RAWHIDE *throws his hat to the floor and sinks dejectedly into a chair by the table; muttering, confusion, etc. continues as lights fade.*)

SCENE 6

The lights come up on the NARRATOR, *seated Stage Right. He will deliver a line and sing another verse of the theme song. Some time will need be consumed as the gang must move from the hideout to the interior of the bank. At the conclusion of the theme, other piano music may be played until the gang is ready for their entrance.*

NARRATOR. Well, the plannin' was behind Ralph Rawlins—and beyond nearly his whole gang; so, like with all their other exploits of crime, the Rawlins gang would trust to sheer dumb luck . . . What other kind of luck *could* they have? (*He sings.*)

A BAD DAY AT GOPHER'S BREATH 23

"There's seven wild men ridin' into our town;
There's trouble a'brewin' it's plain.
And if they don't move on
Without takin' that payroll,
There's gonna be some killin' again . . .
There's gonna be some killin' again."

(*The light fades from the* NARRATOR *and comes up on the interior of the bank. We see the teller, old* COGGINS [*quite decrepit and hard of hearing*], *busily helping a customer, when the door opens and the entire gang wedges in,* RAWHIDE *at the head. He is followed, you'll remember, by* RINGO, DOC, SLEEPY, LAREDO, *and* BRUCE. *The gang looks stupid and lost;* RAWHIDE *agitated.* DOC *moves off to the Right, the rest remain in a clump, and* DOPEY *is conspicuously absent.*)

RAWHIDE. (*In a loud whisper, as will be nearly all the gang's lines.*) Bruce— Cover the window! (BRUCE *spreads his body over the expanse of the window, his back to the audience, trying literally to cover it.* RAWHIDE *shakes his head and moves farther in, the rest all upon his heels. He stops abruptly, and all bump into him. The customer and* COGGINS *look sharply at them.*) Look casual— Relax! (*They all shuffle their feet and whistle simultaneously, except for* DOC, *who looks disgusted as usual.* RAWHIDE *more or less moves them into the teller's line. The customer moves away, exposing* RAWHIDE *to the relentless gaze of* COGGINS, *the teller. Another customer, preferably a lady, moves into the back of the line between* DOC *and* BRUCE *on the Right, and* LAREDO *at the end of the line.* RAWHIDE *puts a damper on the shuffling as:*)
TELLER. (*Demanding.*) Well?
RAWHIDE. (*First staring dumbly at* COGGINS, *then to* RINGO.) The note, the note . . . Where's the note?
RINGO. Dopey's got it, Ralph— You remember.

24   A BAD DAY AT GOPHER'S BREATH

RAWHIDE. I know, but where's Dopey? (RINGO *passes the vital question back, and during the next five lines it must arrive at the end of the line and work its way back to* RINGO. *When* LAREDO *gets it, he turns to* DOC *who ignores him; then he asks the lady who registers hostility. Finally, he asks* BRUCE *who provides the answer over his shoulder. Meanwhile:*)

TELLER. Well can I help you, or not?

RAWHIDE. (*Nervously between the teller and the gang.*) Just a moment, Pops!

TELLER. Eh? . . . Ye say ya want to make a loan? Then ye'll have to go see Miss Phingerdoo, but she ain't here right now. . . . Now go on—move out of the line! We've got *customers* waiting!

RINGO. Somebody here must know, Ralph. *Stall* the teller!

TELLER: (*Overhearing this.*) If ye want to make a withdrawal, why didn't ya say so in the first place?!

RAWHIDE. (*Getting the whispered answer from* RINGO.) He what?? (*An incredulous pause as* RINGO *repeats.*) He fell off his horse?? . . .

TELLER. Well, state yer name. Ye can't withdraw no money less'n I know yer name!

RAWHIDE. (*To* RINGO.) Where? (RINGO *whispers.*) Back at the hideout!? Why didn't someone tell me?? (*The gang looks confused, points, shakes heads, etc.*)

TELLER. Look, sonny— You gonna do yer bankin' er not?

RAWHIDE. No . . . , no, not now. I mean, er, . . . we'll all come back later. (*He turns and begins shoving them backwards toward the door.*)

RINGO. (*Pulling out a cigar.*) Do ya want me to light it now, Ralph?

(RAWHIDE *hits him with his hat, and all back out except* BRUCE, *who is still "covering" the window.* RAWHIDE *re-enters a moment later and corrals* BRUCE, *dragging him out. Lights fade.*)

A BAD DAY AT GOPHER'S BREATH 25

SCENE 7

Lights come up on the NARRATOR, *Stage Right. He may be playing his guitar, receiving accompaniment by the pianist.*

NARRATOR. Well, Rawhide Rawlins, he'd set his mind on capturin' the cash in the Clutzmeyer safe . . . on account of his wantin' so bad to get that potato farm fer his mother. Wasn't about to be deterred by the absence of a note. (*He pauses.*) So, havin' painfully adjusted to the huge chances of human error occurrin' inside of his gang, he once again returned to Gopher's Breath—like the notorious leader that he was—to design a new strategy even more foolproof than the last . . . (*Lights come up on the interior of the bank, while light remains on the* NARRATOR. *It is late afternoon; soft music may be playing.* BAMBI PHINGERDOO *is working Downstage Left as the door opens slowly and* RAWHIDE *sidles in, his eyes scanning everything except her. The* NARRATOR *continues with* RAWHIDE's *business:*) Rawhide enters. The teller, having been released early on account of it bein' Friday, nobody remains in the First Phingerdoo Savings & Trust except the innocent Bambi Phingerdoo. (RAWHIDE *continues to move quietly about the bank, first Upstage Center to the famed safe; he doesn't see* BAMBI. *The* NARRATOR *continues:*) Course the whole time whilst Rawhide was reconnoiterin' the bank an' all, he kept his eyes averted from those of the teller, and so he hadn't yet taken a gander at the banker's beautiful niece. (RAWHIDE *continues Downstage cautiously. He stops at the writing table in the Center and begins jotting down notes—of course, he hasn't seen her, nor she him. Music still plays softly. Then, after a while, moving away from the table, he stumbles on a leg of the table, spilling his notes.*)

26 A BAD DAY AT GOPHER'S BREATH

RAWHIDE. (*Throwing notes and hat to the floor, and forgetting that his mission is secret.*) Oh, . . . (*Moans.*) Dadburn it!!!

BAMBI. (*Noticing him, with some alarm—warranted to be sure.*) Sir, did you drop something? May I assist you?

RAWHIDE. (*Hastily retrieving notes without looking.*) What? . . . Oh, . . . uh, . . . no, just looking, thank you, uh, ma'am. (*Then, and only then, after having picked up a whole pile of notes and stuffing them into his shirt, he notices* BAMBI. *With notes clutched against him, his first furtive glance becomes a double-take, an EXAGGERATED DOUBLE-TAKE. She does like-wise, having come through the gate.*)

BAMBI. (*Clutching her heart, speaking absently.*) Sir, . . . You still have left a piece of your . . . um, . . . wastepaper on the . . . (*She trails off.*)

RAWHIDE. (*Absently, notes falling to the floor one and two at a time.*) Oh, . . . That's all right . . . It's only wastepaper . . . (*This scene is much more comical if* RAWHIDE *has all kinds of paper—twenty to thirty sheets—slowly falling through his hands. The room is now bathed in rosy light; flute music wafts in. They take a step or two toward each other.*)

BAMBI. Then, . . . You're the new custodian . . .

RAWHIDE. No, no, ma'am. I'm a bank . . . robber . . .

BAMBI. (*Taking his outstretched hands in her own, sighing.*) Oh, . . . are you robbing ours . . . ?

RAWHIDE. (*Sighing.*) I . . . think so, uh . . .

BAMBI. (*Supplying her name.*) Bambi.

RAWHIDE. Bambi. (*Lights fade on the bank interior and return to the* NARRATOR.)

NARRATOR. I reckon you could say it was love at first sight. Yes sir, kinda funny when ya chaw on it awhile . . . Rotten Ralph Rawlins, he rode into Gopher's Breath a aimin' to do some bodacious stealin'—but it 'pears it weren't meant to be. One look into

A BAD DAY AT GOPHER'S BREATH 27

those enchantin' eyes, and it was Miss Bambi Phingerdoo who did all the stealin'. Stole Ralph's heart plum away. (*He starts thinking and playing his guitar.*) . . . Hmmm, this turn of events won't sit good with Amos Crutchwaffle's plans for financial security.

SCENE 8

The setting is the interior of the bar. The piano has joined in on the guitar music, and both are now playing a lively number. AMOS *and* BELLE *are at a Downstage table,* RABBIT EARS *is slumped over a Rear table, and the girls and a couple of cowboys are at the bar. The music stops abruptly—on a sour note—as a cowboy, his back festooned with arrows, is propelled through the swinging doors. He staggers in with a stop or two, and after a short pause at the bar, falls to the floor. No one registers any surprise;* BELLE *and* AMOS *fail to notice.*

BARKEEP. (*Leaning over the bar.*) What'll it be, stranger? (*There is a short pause, and the music resumes. All return to basic saloon business. Momentarily,* GENERAL CUSTER *bursts through the door flambuoyantly, and the music again stops. He plants himself just inside the door, expecting applause, or at least attention, and not getting any, readjusts his composure and strides to the bar, absently placing his foot on the body of the man with the arrows in his back.*) What'll it be, stranger?

CUSTER. Stranger? . . . Hardly. (*He looks around.*) George Armstrong Custer here. Commander of the famed Seventh Cavalry . . . At your service, sir. (*He doffs his military cap and bows.* CUSTER *should have shoulder length blond hair or wig, a buckskin jacket, striped military trousers and sword. And, of course, he is mustachioed with a goatee.*)

BARKEEP. (*With some impatience.*) What'll it be, stranger? (*This time, he places the emphasis on "strange."*)

CUSTER. (*Ignoring the implication and continuing.*) . . . on a special personal investigation into alleged hostile Indian movements in the area—largely hogwash, in my estimation . . . Certainly, there has been no evidence *here* of such action. (*He looks around for attention and gets none.*) By the way, my good man, I also seek to procure the services of a trustworthy local as a guide . . . (*He pauses to unfold a road map that he spreads on the bar.*) into the region of the Little Big Horn.

BARKEEP. (*Pausing to think.*) Well, there's old Rabbit Ears, over there in the corner . . .

CUSTER. (*Cutting him off.*) Ah, yes . . . (*He sweeps over to the Indian.*) How fitting, how appropo that a . . . sodden savage should be the unwitting instrument in leading General George Armstrong Custer and the Seventh to their ultimate glory. Come, Rabbit Ears, immortality awaits us. (*He strides out, the Indian following. There is a pause, piano music picks up momentarily, and lights brighten on* AMOS *and* BELLE.)

BELLE. Well, Amos, how are you doing in obtaining the key to Bambi Phingerdoo's heart?

AMOS. Well, Belle . . . (*Pauses.*) Not well . . .

BELLE. Not well? Them's strange words fer the jasper who has broken hearts from here to the border . . .

AMOS. (*Stung a bit—quickly.*) I hear tell she's taken up with a stranger.

BELLE. Cain't figger that out neither—all the time you been spendin' with her.

AMOS. Well, I ain't exactly been sparkin' all the

A BAD DAY AT GOPHER'S BREATH 29

time lately—in fact, that's how I come to thinkin' there's someone else involved here.

BELLE. What *have* ya been doin' then?!

AMOS. (*Ashamed.*) Actually, Belle, . . . I been doin' some . . . (*He becomes inaudible.*) bankin'.

BELLE. WHAT?

AMOS. (*Leaping up and turning left, away fom her.*) Bankin'!

BELLE. Bankin'?

AMOS. Yeah, I been havin' some financial difficulties. (*He pauses.*) . . . And Miss Bambi ain't been real cooperative.

BELLE. What do you mean?

AMOS. I was kinda hopin' you wasn't gonna ask that.

BELLE. Amos, . . . You were sayin' . . . ?

AMOS. (*Sitting down again.*) Well, first off, I asked her fer a loan so's I could buy me some new pistols, on account of how I was gettin' slivvers off'n all the notches on the old ones . . .

BELLE. (*Testily.*) Ya tryin' to win her over er git a low interest rate! Amos, where does this get *us?*

AMOS. I figgered a little negotiatin' would bring us together; she ain't one easy filly to sidle up to socially . . . Some nonsense 'bout me an' violence . . .

BELLE. I cain't imagine the connection. So you asked her fer a loan to buy pistols— Yer a prize, Amos! (*She turns away, shaking her head.*)

AMOS. Mebbe I was a mite hasty with my borrowin'— Looked so handy is all.

BELLE. The handwritin's on the wall, plain an' simple. Cancel yer loan and hang up yer irons. Then you kin get the combination and we kin hightail it across the border.

AMOS. Don't need to cancel the loan. Miss Bambi wouldn't give it to me—said my credit weren't good enough.

BELLE. Oh.

AMOS. It ain't gonna be real easy, Belle. I don't reckon she cottons much to my job neither.

BELLE. Fer Pete sake! What in hell's sheriffin' got to do with winnin' the heart of the lady! Surely she don't object to the law!

AMOS. (*Leaning in.*) Quiet! . . . Cancellin' my loan ain't all she's done— Now she's actin' on foreclosin' the mortgage on the sheriff's office. Now *that told* me there was some other wrangler a'tryin' to cut me out! (*He begins to crumble—desperately*) Belle, . . . she's gonna get the key to my cellblock!!

BELLE. Sounds to me like ya got yer tail between yer legs and are aimin' to call it quits.

AMOS. (*Getting a fierce gleam in his eye and fixing it on* BELLE; *then flinging his chair back a ways and turning Down Front.*) Don't ever talk backin' down to this cayuse, Belle—this here is only a . . . uh, . . . temporary setback.

BELLE. Ya got any idea who this rival of yors is?

AMOS. (*Turning back to her.*) Folks say he looks a lot like Ralph Rawlins.

BELLE. Not the infamous Rotten Rawhide Rawlins, the only man in Gopher's Breath and all points west who can open the Clutzmeyer safe?

AMOS. The very same, Belle. It appears I am not the only man in Gopher's Breath who has designs on Miss Phingerdoo's fortune.

BELLE. Time's runnin' out on ya, Amos. Phidias Phingerdoo is due back the end of this month . . . That bounty hunter, Fat Jack Caldwell may ride in any time to try to cash in on yer hide . . . And, now, if this Rawhide Rawlins is tryin' to get *his* hand in the till, you've got yer work cut out fer ya.

AMOS. (*His pride restored, pounding his fist.*) Never fear, Belle. There ain't a woman born that can resist Amos Crutchwaffle when he's set his mind on it.

BELLE. That may be, Amos, . . . but remember which side yer bisquits are buttered on. Not only that

A BAD DAY AT GOPHER'S BREATH 31

yer my man, but I also hold the secrets of yer past. (*She pauses.*) So play yer game with Bambi Phingerdoo, but only a game, and no more . . . Or you'll wait fer Fat Jack Caldwell by yourself.

SCENE 9

Lights come up on the NARRATOR, Downstage Right.

NARRATOR. Meanwhile, back at the hideout, Bad Bruce has been driven to take desperate action. Working with what most would call "slim pickins," he started doin' something he'd tried to avoid all his like . . . "thinkin,"— Thinkin' on a last try on that Phingerdoo fortune in Gopher's Breath . . . Hunger will do strange things to a man. (*As the lights fade off the NARRATOR, they come up on the interior of the hideout. The state of disorder is the same, except perhaps worse. DOC is on the Upstage cot, LAREDO on the Stage Left cot, BRUCE, on the Upstage side of the table, and SLEEPY, DOPEY, and RINGO, on the Down Stage edge of the table. BRUCE is poring over the plans of the bank. SLEEPY, DOPEY, and RINGO are engaged in a violent fight over some table scraps. BRUCE rises, seeing the anarchy about him.*)

BRUCE. (*Shouting over the fracas.*) All right! All right! Ya ornery galoots— We gonna rob this bank er ain't we?! (*They ignore him.*) Hey! Ya worthless polecats, (*He hesitates, looks, draws his pistol, and fires; there is a very slight diminishing of the hostilities.*)

DOPEY. Uh, . . . What, Bruce?

BRUCE. I think I got this cussed thing figgered out . . . Where we went wrong was we didn't have enough . . . stragg-eddy . . . (*They all look at each other.*)

SLEEPY. . . . Right, uh, . . . Bruce.

32 A BAD DAY AT GOPHER'S BREATH

Doc. What you been doin'— Readin' a dictionary? (BRUCE *whirls on him. The rest plug their ears, duck, etc.*)

BRUCE. (*After a long pause, sensing he knows something that has eluded* Doc.) We can't jes go a'bustin' in there like we did that other time— Rawhide was all wrong— That looks too suspicious.

DOPEY. What *else* can we do?

SLEEPY. (*To* DOPEY.) You remember! That one time in Socorro we didn't— We decided to wait till the loot was bein' hauled out of the safe to move it to Alburquerque . . .

DOPEY. When?

RINGO. (*Absorbed in it.*) The time you dropped yer pistol and damn near shot yer toe off.

DOPEY. Oh, yeah! When we got held up by them other fellers what beat us to the bank . . .

RINGO. (*Slapping his knee.*) That there one almost tops yer missin' the last job!

DOPEY. An' the time ol' Bill gone an' left me when we left the horses to rob the Powder River stage!

SLEEPY. (*Excited.*) Sure is pure enjoyable funnin' about the good ol' times . . .

BRUCE. (*Interrupting, shouting.*) Hold it! You was listenin' to me! I got this all planned out . . .

Doc. (*Sarcasm.*) Damn! I hope I don't need no pencil and paper. I plum forgot!

BRUCE. (*Missing* Doc's *intent.*) No, no. It's purty simple.

Doc. Really? I'd have never guessed.

BRUCE. (*Continuing.*) I know what we was missin'.

RINGO. What's that, Bruce?

BRUCE. (*Beaming.*) Disguises . . . !

THE GANG. Disguises??!

BRUCE. Yeah, . . . disguises . . . That's what we was missin'. We can't jus' go bustin' in there lookin' like a gang of ordinary outlaws.

Doc. Huh . . . ? (*Takes a toothpick from his*

A BAD DAY AT GOPHER'S BREATH 33

mouth.) . . . This ain't *never* been no ordinary gang.

BRUCE. You fellas jus don't pay him no mind. He ain't got no head fer stragg-eddy and newfangled outlawin'. (*Gets a scornful look from* Doc.)

LAREDO. What kinda disguises, Bruce?

BRUCE. Oh, all kinds. Like, uh, . . . townsfolk. One of us could be a preacher; they're always good.

DOPEY. Yeah, Good!

BRUCE. And another couple of ya could be little ol' ladies . . .

RINGO. I ain't gonna be no lady!

LAREDO. Me neither!

BRUCE. (*Enraged at disloyalty.*) Oh, yes ya are! (*He pulls his pistol.*) Ya worthless varmints!!

LAREDO. Right, Bruce!

RINGO. Anything ya say!

BRUCE. (*Settling back down, gun on the table.*) Well, since we're agreed on our disguises, now we'll go over the rest of the plan. Let's see now . . . Now, first, me an' Rawhide will go in . . . And we'll go to the teller's window; then comes Laredo, Ringo, Sleepy, and Dopey— Doc is gonna cover the window! Ha, ha, ha! (Doc *ignores this; the others wait for the confrontation.*) An' then, . . . (*They all lean in.*) When Dopey comes up by me an' Rawhide and waves the little note, then Ringo and Laredo, you's rush over that little fence . . . (*He points.*) and knock everybody down. (*He finishes beaming, all excited.*)

SLEEPY. Will we recognize Dopey, or will we be surprised?

DOC. Oh, you'll be surprised, I expect. I have gotta say, Bruce, this is a first-rate plan . . .

RINGO. (*Admiringly.*) Yeah, . . . Do I get to light up a cigar, Bruce?

DOC. One other question. You've undoubtedly invented a master stroke of strategy. You'll need to name it . . . Maybe, the Bruce Plan. No. . . . Or the Bad Bruce Plan. Er, maybe just . . . the Bad Plan . . .

BRUCE. (*Catching on—enraged.*) I knowed you was jus' funnin'!! I knowed it!

DOC. (*Turning to* RAWHIDE *as the latter enters.*) Bout time ya got here; the town fool just about took over yer gang. (*Then, so all can hear.*) What's the lowdown on the bank?

BRUCE. (*Stepping on the end of* DOC's *line.*) Turn around, ya skunk so's I kin kill ya!!

RAWHIDE. (*Really irritated though not knowing exactly why.*) Bruce, you got something you gotta say?!

BRUCE. Well, uh, . . . uh, . . . I . . .

RAWHIDE. Then shut up an' let me say my piece, all right?

BRUCE. (*Trailing off.*) I reckon ya kin hear my plan afterwards . . .

RAWHIDE. It's gonna be real tough. Fer one thing, I, . . . uh, . . . heard that most of that payroll gold may be, uh, . . . moved outa the Clutzmeyer safe anytime— Soon!

LAREDO. More reason fer hittin' it right away— We're ready an' itchin' to go, Boss.

RAWHIDE. (*Hastily thinking, his romance his only real concern.*) I also heard that uh, . . . they're putting a guard— Double Guard!— Triple Guard!! on the loot till the company collects it. Remember, there's still Amos Crutchwaffle. It'll mean a lot of shootin'. He runs a tight town . . .

SLEEPY. (*Eagerly.*) No it won't!

RAWHIDE. Won't what?

DOPEY. No, we're gonna have . . . stragg eddy. —We're gonna be ladies . . .

RAWHIDE. (*Looking incredulous.*) . . . No, no, uh, . . . I think we ought to go to Santa Fe.

THE GANG. (*In unison.*) We can't afford to!!

BRUCE. It's gotta be Gopher's Breath.

SLEEPY. Yeah, Gopher's Breath.

DOPEY, RINGO. Yeah, Gopher's Breath!

A BAD DAY AT GOPHER'S BREATH 35

(RAWHIDE *throws his hat down and sinks into a chair to lean on his elbows dejectedly. The conclusion of Scene 9 is a convenient place for an intermission.*)

SCENE 10

Honky-tonk music is playing in the darkness to permit the gang to "clear out" of the hideout with little distraction. Then, lights come up on the interior of the saloon. AMOS CRUTCHWAFFLE *is drunk and unconscious at the Up Right table,* RABBIT EARS *has returned from the Little Big Horn and is in his stupor at the Down Right table. A few cowboys are at the bar or are playing cards at the Down Left table. At a designated cue, the saloon girls,* APRIL, MAY, *and* JUNE—*who have been milling about—form a chorus line and perform a lively rendition of an old "favorite." The song may be done to any convenient tune, as long as it builds to a big finish. The ending of the song is hailed by hats thrown, whistles, and cheers.* AMOS *and* RABBIT EARS *fail to stir. As all begin to return to basic saloon business, an extraneous sound is heard. As it approaches from down the street, one can detect strains of "Bringing in the Sheaves." A cowboy goes to the door to investigate.*

FOURTH COWBOY. Whut in tarnation is that there ruckus yonder in the street? (*Two ladies push open the swinging doors, flattening him;* PANDORA CRUTCHWAFFLE, *with mallet, hatchet, or similar weapon, fills the doorway. There is a pause; cowboys react with horror, or at least dismay, and shrink away.* PANDORA *strides over the prone cowboy and to the bar, followed by ladies wielding a bass drum, tambourine, coronet, and various weapons. The ladies scatter a bit.*)

36 A BAD DAY AT GOPHER'S BREATH

BARKEEP. (*With no inflection.*) What'll it be, stranger?

PANDORA. (*Her voice steadily rising to thunder.*) What'll it be? What'll it be!! . . . I'll tell you what it'll be, . . . you nefarious dispensor of the demon rum. (*She turns Downstage Center after backing* BARKEEP *up.*) It will be a glorious day, brothers and sisters, when all such dark, despicable dens of degradation are brought low and stricken from the face of the earth! (*There are a few "amens," drum beats, etc.*) Yes, only when the doors of all such polluted parlors of perfidy have been barred and shuttered can the forces of John Barleycorn be put to rout. —Only then can the broken family be reunited; only then will the neglected child, crying for sustenance, know an end to its pitiful want . . . !! (*There are prolonged cheers, "Amen's," "Praise be's," "Hallelujah's," and musical noises. At this cacophony,* AMOS *recoils, falls backward, and leaps out of his chair, kicking the chair away, drawing his pistols, and firing blindly into the crowd. The "regulars" all duck for cover, but the temperance ladies just stand their ground. Two cowboys catch stray bullets and "bite the dust."*)

AMOS. (*Drunkenly leaning, guns in hand.*) Whaa's goin' on here?! —What are ya doin'!

PANDORA. Indeed! What am I doing! Look what you have done in league with the Devil!

AMOS. (*Searching.*) Whut?

PANDORA. (*A step toward him.*) I'll tell you what you have done! —You have *interrupted* me! (*She and everyone else have disregarded the two corpses.*)

AMOS. Lady, . . . I done that by myself! (*There are gasps, foul looks;* AMOS *staggers and catches himself.*) Now you jes . . .

PANDORA. (*Interrupting.*) Silence, you heathen! Have you no courtesy?

FIRST COWBOY. Careful, lady. Don't you know who that is?

PANDORA. What? That? Merely another unfortunate wretch, a victim of his own insatiable thirsts and unnatural appetites.

FIRST COWBOY. Unnatural ain't the word fer it, lady— That's Sheriff Amos Crutchwaffle, the second most feared man in the West!

PANDORA. (*Incredulously.*) Amos Crutchwaffle . . . ! Can it be? My own long-lost, ne'er-do-well brother . . . ? (*There are a lot of gasps; this even surprises some of the usual customers.*)

AMOS. Pandora? Pandora, is that you, Pandora? (*His vision is more than blurred—he staggers to her.*) My own long-gone but not forgotten elder spinster sister . . . ?

PANDORA. Oh, shame. Oh, degradation; my own kith and kin, a sodden drunkard adrift on the sea of inebriation, cast into the abyss of intemperance—another hapless victim of the demon rum . . . ! (*She suddenly grabs him.*) Shame! Shame and fie, Amos! Your loathsome presence has brought dishonor on the Crutchwaffle name.

AMOS. (*Pointing with a pistol.*) Now, see here. (*All duck.*) Yor presence here ain't *exactly* doin' me no honor neither!

PANDORA. (*Advancing on him.*) Honor? What would you know of honor, . . . you whelp?!

AMOS. (*Leaning backwards.*) Hold there! I can't abide shootin' women—even less my own kin, but . . . ! (*He tips back, collapsing Center Stage, in a stupor.*)

PANDORA. (*Changing her attitude as she bends to help him up.*) Come, Amos. Blood is thicker than water; lift your head up. . . . What a testimonial you shall be, brother, and— (*Turning to the ladies.*) what a star in our crown, girls! (*Lots of cheers, etc.*) Come. We will leave here together!

AMOS. (*Still holding pistols as* PANDORA *leads him Downstage Center.*) But, Pandora—

PANDORA. (*Brandishing her hammer and holding*

him up.) Do not despair, Amos; every cloud has a silver lining, I see the light at the end of the tunnel; it is always darkest before the dawn . . .

AMOS. But, Pandora— (PANDORA *administers a "gently" chastising blow with her hammer—Whacko! * AMOS *is an inch shorter; his pistols now droop.*)

PANDORA. We must make hay while the sun shines; virtue is its own reward; there is a pot of gold at the end of every rainbow.

AMOS. But, Pandora— (PANDORA *hits him again, and most of the saloon clientele winces with the blow.* AMOS *sinks lower, and with guns still in hand, staggers Left to the Downstage Left table and falls into the Stage Left chair. There is a nearly empty prop bottle on the table.*)

PANDORA. (*Crossing to him, putting a hand on his shoulder.*) Come, Amos, it is time to cease your doleful tramp into intoxication and ruin . . . (*She picks up the bottle and waves it.*) I will lead you on your upward climb toward sobriety . . . (*He repeatedly reaches to grab the bottle, she repeatedly moving it out of his grasp.*) toward ransom from the enslaving grasp of distilled spirits. Surely now, Amos, you can see that it is not too late, all is not lost—

AMOS. Gol dang it, Pandora! All I kin see is that there bottle. Now give it to me!

PANDORA. All right, unrepentant son of Lucifer— Have it!! (*She breaks it over his head. He raises himself a bit higher, takes a step Right, in front of her, and falls to the floor. She stares at him for an instant, and then wiping her hands of the whole business, moves Center Stage.*) Well, there's more work here.

BELLE. (*Coming to meet* PANDORA *from the stairs she has just descended; there is a pistol in her hand.*) I reckon you've done about all the work yer gonna do today in these parts.

PANDORA. (*To the crowd.*) And who is this brazen hussie?

A BAD DAY AT GOPHER'S BREATH   39

BELLE. The name's Belle Durham, and I'm the owner of this here establishment. You may as well put up them hatchets and hammers and march right on outa here, cause you ain't doin' no bar-bustin' here today.

PANDORA. (*Defiantly, but backing right a step.*) How dare you!! (BELLE *cocks the pistol hammer.*) Very well. . . . You have not seen the last of me. (*She turns and begins to drag* AMOS *out by the collar.*)

BELLE. Where ya goin' with him?

PANDORA. He is my brother, and I am rescuing him—

BELLE. Well, he's my man, and I figger it's high time you leave off usin' him fer a railroad spike . . . (*Pauses.*) Now, just beat yer big bass drum on outa here.

(PANDORA *takes a menacing half step toward* BELLE, *who then aims the pistol unmistakably at* PANDORA. PANDORA *stops abruptly, turns, wheeling over to the swinging doors, looks around at her cohorts, and, throwing her head up in a haughty gesture, departs with a flourish. The others follow, and "Bringing in the Sheaves" is again heard in the distance, The lights fade.*)

SCENE 11

The setting is the interior of the bank, in the evening past closing time. The lights first come up on the NARRATOR, *seated Stage Right.*

NARRATOR. Later that same night, as his gang slept, dangerous Rawhide Rawlins once more snuck into Gopher's Breath. Keepin' to the shadows, he made his way to the bank where a longin' Bambi Phingerdoo awaited him. (*When the lights go up on the bank interior,* BAMBI *is behind the teller's window. There is a special, secret knock on the door; she rushes anxiously to open it. She stops short . . .*)

BAMBI. Is that you, Ralph?
RAWHIDE. (*In a loud whisper.*) Yes!!
BAMBI. What?
RAWHIDE. Yes, of course it is! Who else would it be?— It's 9 O'clock!
BAMBI. But it is not the prescribed knock that we agreed upon . . .
RAWHIDE. Bambi, we can't be meetin' like this!! Let me in!
BAMBI. (*Hesitantly, then unlocking the door and flinging it open.*) Yes, uh, . . . of course, Ralph. (*He rushes in; they both look furtively outside, and she locks the door again.*) Oh, Ralph, I thought you would never come.
RAWHIDE. Neither did I. I thought they'd never go to sleep.
BAMBI. They all went to sleep before you came?
RAWHIDE. Yeah. I bedded 'em all down an' read to 'em . . . 'bout old train robberies an' all.
BAMBI. Well, the only thing that matters now is that we're together at last. (*They cross to the bench hand-in-hand.*)
RAWHIDE. Oh, Bambi.
BAMBI. Oh, Ralph.
RAWHIDE. Oh, Bambi.
BAMBI. Oh, Ralph, tell me, Ralph— Tell me what I long to hear. Tell me how you have talked to your gang and convinced them not to rob my uncle's bank and no longer lead a life of crime . . . Ralph?
RAWHIDE. (*Looking downcast, at the floor; shuffling his feet.*) Oh! . . . , Bambi . . .
BAMBI. (*She is shaken.*) You mean . . .
RAWHIDE. Oh, Bambi, what'll I do?
BAMBI. (*Recovering bravely—the spunky little gal that she is.*) Ralph—if your gang is not to be deterred, there's only one thing left for us to do . . . (*Pauses.*) You must go to the Sheriff and give yourself up— Throw yourself on his mercy.

A BAD DAY AT GOPHER'S BREATH 41

RAWHIDE. (*Leaping up and pacing Right.*) You don't mean Amos Crutchwaffle! —Not him! He'd shoot first and ask questions later—soon's I showed my face!

BAMBI. (*To him.*) But if you went unarmed . . . ?

RAWHIDE. He'd still shoot me, purely outa meanness.

BAMBI. Oh, Ralph, do you then think that honest Amos is not the kind man and gentleman that he appears to be?

RAWHIDE. Holy cow, Bambi! Why do ya think he's the second most feared man in the West? Beneath that badge beats the heart of a cold-blooded killer and a thief besides. I ain't so sure that he hasn't got his sights set on gettin' that payroll fer hisself—one way or t'uther. I got a feelin' he's gonna need some travelin' money soon.

BAMBI. Why, what do you mean?

RAWHIDE. Amos Crutchwaffle is a man with a price on his head and word has it that Fat Jack Caldwell is riding in to collect.

BAMBI. Not Fat Jack Caldwell, the most feared man in the West?!!

RAWHIDE. None other, Bambi.

BAMBI. (*Pausing, thoughtfully.*) Then, if we can't trust Sheriff Crutchwaffle, then . . . (*Pause.*) you must go directly to the Governor himself!

RAWHIDE. (*Bewildered.*) The Governor? What'll I say to *him*?

BAMBI. You must explain to him your change of heart— Offer to aid the forces of true law and order in foiling the intended larceny. Declare your honest and true intentions, and, (*Her voice rising in hope.*) you may receive pardon, Ralph!

RAWHIDE. But do you really think there's a chance?

BAMBI. Yes, of course. After all, you've never killed anyone, have you?

RAWHIDE. (*With some hesitation.*) No . . . Actually, I've never even shot anyone . . .

BAMBI. (*Amazed.*) You have never shot at anyone, Ralph?

RAWHIDE. Oh, I've shot *at* them . . . Lord knows I've tried, Bambi . . . (*He hangs his head in shame.*)

BAMBI. Oh, Ralph . . . (*She pauses; then, in excitement—*) Ralph, this means you're only wanted for robbery!

RAWHIDE. Yeah, but there's a whole parcel of them!

BAMBI. Oh, dear, Ralph . . . What of all the money you've stolen?

RAWHIDE. All . . . , Bambi?

BAMBI. Yes, Ralph. What happened to it?

RAWHIDE. Why, I have it right here. (*Without guile—the straightforward lad that he is—he reaches into his shirt to pull a small leather pouch out to show* BAMBI.)

BAMBI. (*Not seeing the pouch.*) Where?

RAWHIDE. Here, here in my hand!

BAMBI. (*Pointing and confused.*) In there? Why, how much is it?

RAWHIDE. (*Proudly, in spite of all this.*) $37.52.

BAMBI. Is that all that's left, Ralph? (*She is crestfallen.*)

RAWHIDE. (*More disappointed.*) This is all there is— All there ever was! We never spent a dime . . . I've saved every penny for Mom!

BAMBI. (*More incredulous.*) But . . . , how do you all live . . . ? What do you all do?

RAWHIDE. (*Turning away, shame-faced and mumbling.*) Oh, odd jobs . . . A little here, a little there . . .

BAMBI. (*Recovering.*) Ralph . . . , this is wonderful!

RAWHIDE. (*Indignantly.*) You think it's wonderful? I ain't never told anyone before, but me and the boys have had a helluva tough time of it, Bambi . . . An' the boys been purty patient, too . . .

BAMBI. No, Ralph— This all means you can make full restitution for your crimes, and if you only aid in the foiling of the robbery at the bank, you're sure to receive full pardon . . . Oh, Ralph . . .

A BAD DAY AT GOPHER'S BREATH 43

RAWHIDE. (*Taking her hand.*) Oh, Bambi . . .
BAMBI. Oh, Ralph . . . (*They embrace as lights fade.*)

SCENE 12

Lights come up on the NARRATOR, *Downstage Right.*

NARRATOR. And so Ralph and Bambi traveled to the capital and met with the Governor, and a bargain was struck. If Ralph would return all his ill-gotten booty, and if he would aid the territorial marshall in capturing his gang, he would earn his pardon. Hard as it was for Ralph to leave behind his life-long career of crime, his love for Bambi was all-consuming. And so the stage was set for the final chapter in the saga of the Rawlins gang. Ralph thought he held all the cards, but there were two jokers in the deck. First, the plucky Bambi Phingerdoo, unwilling to place an unsuspecting employee in a position of possible danger, had herself taken the place of the bank's teller. And, second, the territorial marshall, held up by a washout, had telegraphed the local sheriff—Amos Crutchwaffle—to let him in on the plan. Amos was only too happy to oblige the marshall and stand in for him. For Ralph and Bambi, it was the beginning of a bad day in Gopher's Breath.

Lights reveal the interior of the bank. BAMBI PHINGERDOO *is working Down Left, and fails to note the entrance of the gang. They all enter in a bunch, and come to stand in the Center of the bank, save* DOC, *who stands, detached, to their Right, and* RAWHIDE, *who stands Left, near the teller's window. The rest are grouped about* DOPEY *and* BAD BRUCE. DOPEY, RINGO, *and* SLEEPY *are wearing dresses, etc. over their "normal" attire, and their weapons over the dresses;* BRUCE *wears a clerical collar that shows through an overcoat. All, including the "ladies" continue to wear their cowboy hats and bandanas.*

DOPEY. (*In a stage whisper.*) I feel awful silly, Bruce . . . Do I have to go through with this?

BRUCE. You heard what Rawhide said— They's got guards all over this place, so's we need us a hostage. Now do like I told ya!

DOPEY. (*After a disgusted look at* BRUCE.) Oh, my . . . Oh— (BRUCE *hits him with his hat, and* DOPEY'S VOICE *goes falsetto.*) I mean, oh, my, oh, my; I think I feel faint!

BRUCE. (*In an awkward, extra-polite way.*) Oh, dear, oh, dear . . . Perhaps a glass of water would help . . . Does anyone have a glass of water for this poor lady? (*All look around, hoping for assistance, except for* Doc *who is disgusted, and* RAWHIDE *who appears edgy.* DOPEY *continues.*)

DOPEY. Oh, my, oh, my; I think I feel faint— (*To* BRUCE.) Am I doin' good, Bruce?

BRUCE. Shut up and keep actin', ya stupid!

RINGO, SLEEPY, LAREDO, and then BRUCE. (*All joining in—a chorus.*) Oh, my, a glass of water . . . Does anyone have a . . . etc.

BAMBI. (*She momentarily comes to the teller's window, her eyes searching out her beloved, but he fails to see her as his back is turned.*) Oh! . . . Ah, ah, I have some water right back here. I'll get it. (*She exits Stage Left.*)

BRUCE. (*To the others.*) All right. Git ready now. When she gits out here, we grab her! . . . And watch out for the guards! (BAMBI *returns through the gate with the water, and* RAWHIDE, *with the others, turns to her.*)

RAWHIDE. Bambi! (*The gang turns to him.*)
BAMBI. Ralph! (*The gang turns to her.*)
RAWHIDE. But what are you doing here?

A BAD DAY AT GOPHER'S BREATH 45

Doc. (*Smelling a rat.*) Hey! What is this?

RAWHIDE. All right, boys—hold it right there. Don't make any moves ya might regret. (*On the line, he draws his pistol and motions the gang toward the teller's cage fence on Stage Left;* BAMBI *is left more or less in the middle with* RAWHIDE *Right Center.*)

Doc. If this is some kind of doublecross, it ain't gonna be us doin' the regrettin'.

BRUCE. Ralph, you ain't aimin' to keep all the loot fer yerself . . . ?

RAWHIDE. There ain't gonna be no loot, boys— (*He pauses.*) Cause there ain't gonna be no robbery . . . Bambi, you get on back behind that teller's cage. (*She does so.*)

Doc. (*Getting real nasty.*) I don't know what yer tryin' to pull, but it 'pears to me there's only one of you tellin' me there *ain't* gonna be no robbery, and there's six of us sayin' there *is*—

RINGO, LAREDO, BRUCE. Yeah! (*They fan out menacingly into a semi-circle, their hands near their guns.* DOPEY *and* SLEEPY *fumble with their dresses.*)

RAWHIDE. Stand easy, boys. We don't want no unnecessary fireworks . . . , cause maybe the odds ain't as good as you think. (*Then louder, after a pause.*) All right, Marshall, reckon it's time you made yer move! (*The gang all looks around, amazed and bewildered; there is a long pause, a really long one.*) . . . Marshall . . . ?

LAREDO. I don't see no marshall!

Doc. Me neither— Let's take him, boys! (*There is another short pause, and then* AMOS CRUTCHWAFFLE *kicks in the door.*)

AMOS. (*After stopping in the doorway.*) Marshall couldn't make it . . . Will I do?

DOPEY. Who *is* that? (RAWHIDE *has now realized that something is amiss, and turns to face the guns of* AMOS CRUTCHWAFFLE.)

RAWHIDE. Amos Crutchwaffle!

AMOS. (*Mockingly.*) Well, ain't this a sight fer sore eyes. Hard to tell if this is the notorious Rawlins gang robbin' a bank . . . , or a Saturday afternoon ladies' social!

DOC. Never figgered you to throw in with a bushwhackin' polecat like this un, Rawhide!

RAWHIDE. Darn it! I mighta known it . . . I mighta known! First time I set out *not* to rob a bank, and something like this happens.

SLEEPY. (*He pats* RAWHIDE *on the shoulder.*) Gosh, Rawhide, we understand.

DOPEY, RINGO. We do?

AMOS. (*He lights a long black cigar.*) Yeah, Rawlins, it's too bad, too bad. Things is turnin' out a whole helluva lot better fer me than theys gonna turn out fer you.

BAMBI. (*Over the fence and through the gang.*) But Ralph was trying to *stop* the robbery—he's giving up his life of crime!

AMOS. Oh, he's giving up somethin' all right . . . But ain't nobody gonna know what— That'll just be our little secret.

BAMBI. (*Bravely.*) But he's going to get a pardon.

RINGO, DOPEY. (*To the others.*) Is he?

SLEEPY. (*To* RAWHIDE.) Are ya, Rawhide?

AMOS. No, fellas, all he's gonna git is a bullet. (*He pauses, during which time the gang members begin to show signs of real agitation and fear; then, continuing.*) Unless, of course, you an' me, Miss Bambi, can work out some kinda deal. Picture this, if you will: Seems the infamous Rawlins gang rode into Gopher's Breath to git the payroll out of the Clutzmeyer safe in the First Phingerdoo Savings and Trust. The sheriff surprised 'em all in the act, however, and in the gunfight which naturally followed, the sheriff killed the whole gang in the course of duty— (*During a pause here, near panic breaks out in the gang.*) But mebbe, jes mebbe, the leader of the gang, Rawhide Rawlins, managed to git away . . .

A BAD DAY AT GOPHER'S BREATH   47

RAWHIDE. What are you gettin' at, Crutchwaffle?

AMOS. You see, Miss Bambi, it's all in yer hands now. Bein' the sheriff, I'm bound by law to shoot down all these outlaws, but if you was to see yer way clear to—

RAWHIDE. (*Interrupting.*) You just hold on there, you—

AMOS. Hang onta yor reins, hombre! (AMOS *hisses this and cocks both his pistols.*) It's yor right to go on breathin' that me and the little lady are discussin' ... Now, Miss Bambi, as I was sayin,' if you could see yer way clear to open that there safe, and then, say, ride along south with me and the money, why then, jes' mebbe yor sweetheart here might escape with his life.

RAWHIDE. You'll never get away with this, Crutchwaffle, I'll hunt you down if it's the last thing I do!

AMOS. I doubt that, Rawlins— You see, you'll be too busy dodging all the posses that'll be on ya fer stealin' the payroll an' fer kidnappin' the banker's niece ... Ain't nobody gonna suspect me fer this here crime over you, badman—an' there ain't gonna be no witnesses ... But it's a damn sight better'n bein' buried. (*He pauses.*) Well, what will it be, Miss Bambi?

RAWHIDE. Don't trust him, Bambi— His word ain't no good. Once he's got the money and you, I won't be no more'n buzzard bait!

DOC. Well, I ain't waitin' around fer you all to make up yer minds. Git the light, Bruce!!

(BRUCE *shoots the lights out, and* BAMBI *and* RALPH *escape Down Left as the fight begins. In the darkness, we see only the flash of gunfire as* AMOS *guns down* RINGO, LAREDO, *and* DOPEY *near the teller's cage, and* SLEEPY *takes a dive off the stage. The shootout ends for* DOC *and* BRUCE *near* AMOS' *feet. At the conclusion of the carnage,* AMOS *lights a lamp to reveal the scene, then looks around for*

A BAD DAY AT GOPHER'S BREATH

BAMBI *and* RAWHIDE, *and exits Down Left. Lights fade.*)

SCENE 13

Lights come up on the interior of the saloon; inside are two or three cowboys, the drunken Indian, BAR-KEEP, and the girls. Music is playing. The music suddenly stops and everyone wheels to face the doors or ducks as AMOS enters and hesitates at the door, guns in hand. Then he rushes to the bar, looks over it, shoving patrons and girls out of the way; he searches Down Left, and returns to face the audience in the Center for his line.

AMOS. All right, Rawlins! I know you come in here— Come out and face me man to man! I'll find ya sooner or later anyhow! (*After a slight pause,* RAWHIDE *appears on the stairway landing; all move out of the line of fire.*)

RAWHIDE. You won't have to look far, Crutchwaffle— I'm right here! (AMOS *whirls, guns aimed; he holsters them and backs Down Right a step.* RAWHIDE *comes to the bottom of the stairs as* BAMBI *is now on the landing.*)

BAMBI. No, Ralph! You mustn't—!

RAWHIDE. A man can't keep runnin' forever, Bambi.

BAMBI. But, Ralph, you're no match for him— He will kill you if you draw!

AMOS. He's got no choice. . . . If'n he's a man.

BAMBI. It's not too late, Ralph. Put away your pistol, turn and walk away— The sheriff wouldn't shoot you in the back! We'll yet find a new life somewhere . . . Ralph . . . ?

AMOS. Afraid yer wrong, Ma'am—dead wrong in this case. I kin shoot this criminal jest as legal as not . . . , an' I aim to do that. (*Both men remain*

A BAD DAY AT GOPHER'S BREATH 49

poised and tense; everyone else has ducked nearly out of sight.)

RAWHIDE. We're up a box canyon, Bambi. I don't reckon it's any use talkin' . . . I *do* regret havin' to kill fer you and Mom though.

AMOS. I'll be sure and send my condolences— I'm callin' ya, Badman! (AMOS *walks backward toward the door; both he and* RAWHIDE *are ready to draw.* BAMBI *awaits trembling at the bottom of the stairs. Suddenly, in through the door steps none other than* FAT JACK CALDWELL. *The doors slam back against him, propelling him into the room.* FAT JACK *must be the antithesis of all that's heretofore been said of him. He is pencil-thin, blond, mustachioed and pale; he wears white fringed buckskin, white, furry chaps, and red-white-and-blue boots. His hat and twin pistols are too small, almost child-like, and he speaks with a high, thin voice.*)

BARKEEP, BAMBI, RAWHIDE, ET AL. FAT JACK CALDWELL!!

BARKEEP. . . . The most feared man in the West! (AMOS *swings around, forgetting* RAWHIDE. *He is visibly shaken.*)

FAT JACK. (*His hands resting on his pistols.*) It's been a long time since Tombstone, Amos Crutchwaffle.

AMOS. I figgered you'd show up sooner or later, Caldwell.

FAT JACK. Well, you know me, old horse. I never give 'em up so long as they keep a smell about 'em. . . . And I might say, you have, Sheriff!

AMOS. Yor worse'n them buzzards out yonder on the trail!

FAT JACK. Never you mind me, Horse. Instead let's change the subject— I hope yer tarred of livin', ya lop-eared coyote.

AMOS. If'n any dyin's gonna be done, it's gonna be you doin' it, ya ornery varmint.

FAT JACK. Oh, yeah. The way I see it, you rustled

yer last hereford, ya tightened yer last cinch, branded yer last stray, dry-gulched yer last cowpoke . . .

AMOS. (*Interrupting.*) —Says you. You done cocked yer last Winchester, poked yer last cow, escaped yer last noose, downed yer last rotgut . . . (*Most of the saloon crowd has now relaxed a bit;* RAWHIDE *has joined* BAMBI *as just two more spectators to the drama*).

FAT JACK. Come off it, Amos Crutchwaffle— You know which one of us is the most feared man in the West!

AMOS. Bein' the most feared is one thing— Won't know who's the fastest til the smoke clears.

FAT JACK. Then let's cut the palaverin'! (*They begin to circle each other, waiting for an advantage. Both are crouching low; when they slow down, everyone in the saloon ducks.* BELLE *has now appeared on the landing of the stairway.*)

AMOS. (*Ready to draw; he has now worked his way to Downstage Right, and* FAT JACK *to Upstage Left— everyone ducks for an instant until the lines begin again.*) Make yer move, Fat Jack!

FAT JACK. Yer stallin', Crutchwaffle! —Fill your hand! (*They do a long tense look at each other and begin moving again,* AMOS *to Upstage Right and* FAT JACK *to Downstage Left. They stop, as if to draw. All duck again momentarily.*)

AMOS. Who's stallin'?! Stand still and slap leather, ya yella sidewinder!

FAT JACK. Yella! Yella, is it! I'll show ya who's yella, ya tinhorn! Draw!!

AMOS. You draw, ya lowdown coyote! I'm waitin' on ya, an' I ain't got all night!

FAT JACK. You sure as hell ain't . . . You ain't got but a few seconds! (*They exchange another mean, ugly look and move again. This time,* AMOS *moves until his back is to the stairs, and* JACK *moves to Downstage Right.*)

A BAD DAY AT GOPHER'S BREATH 51

AMOS. I got no more time to waste on the likes o' you.
FAT JACK. (*Fairly screaming.*) It's *me* what's wastin' time!!
AMOS. (*Equally so.*) It ain't!! —Me and the banker's niece got an appointment in Mexico! (*On this line the audience will see that* BELLE *now wipes a tear from her eye with one hand that holds a handkerchief while the other plainly holds a pistol. —She knows the score.*)
FAT JACK. Appointment! You only got an appointment with mah shootin' irons, ya weak-kneed choir boy— (*Pauses.*) Come on, Crutchwaffle— This IS IT!!

(*The two stand motionless for a moment; all in the saloon duck, fearing the hail of lead that will now burst forth. Then—just as they begin their respective motions to their guns—*BELLE, *in anguish, raises her pistol and fires once, hitting* AMOS *squarely in the back.* AMOS *lurches Downstage, and* FAT JACK *looks dumbfounded, stupidly checking to see if his guns are still holstered or not.*)

AMOS. (*Pausing mid-lurch, to* FAT JACK.) Ya got me! —Fastest draw I ever seen! I never even got a chance to clear leather! (FAT JACK *is still looking around, checking himself; then* AMOS *turns and sees* BELLE *and her weapon.*) Belle, honey—ya mean it was you? . . . But why?
BELLE. (*Coming toward* AMOS.) I reckon I knowed fer a long time it'd have to come to somethin' like this. You couldn't help but see a storm a-brewin'. You were plannin' on cuttin' me out . . . I could see it in your eyes. (*Perhaps on this line, the saloon girls could add mood music.*) When a man looks at a woman the way you been lookin' at Bambi Phingerdoo, his mind's on more'n just money . . .

AMOS. (*Staggering to fall into* FAT JACK'S *arms.*) But Belle, ain't I always played ya straight? . . .

BELLE. You could never deal off the top of the deck, Amos— Even when ya tried . . .

AMOS. I wouldn't have just left ya cold, Belle. I always planned on leavin' you yor share of the money a'fore I rode off . . .

BELLE. But I wanted both you *and* the money, Amos . . .

AMOS. (*Rising off* FAT JACK, *and loudly.*) But now ya don't get either one!!

BELLE. (*A trifle irritated as well.*) Ain't you forgettin' Tombstone, Amos? Ain't you forgettin' you got a big price on yer head? I figger that there bounty oughta just buy my way outa Gopher's Breath fer good.

FAT JACK. (*Remembering.*) The bounty. (*He drops* AMOS.) Now I remember!

AMOS. (*Struggling toward the Upstage Right table.*) You mean you did it just for the money, Belle?

BELLE. No. I jest got off before I got throwed . . . You were my man, Amos, but you were doin' me wrong.

AMOS. (*Staggering to* BELLE.) You cain't get (*He coughs.*) off'n this kinda life, Belle. —What else could ya do? (*He lurches to the bar.*)

BELLE. (*A step Downstage.*) I got my sights set on a little farm somewheres. I been hankerin' to plant some roots and mebbe grow myself a little garden.

AMOS. It's a little late now, Belle . . . But I could've helped ya settle. You know ya can't do it alone now.

BELLE. I'll find help somewhere. —Ya can't tighten up on the reins when there's a new life out there a'waitin' on ya . . . I kin buy me a hired hand with the bounty money if need be.

RAWHIDE. (*Interrupting and taking a step Downstage also, still hand-in-hand with his sweetheart.*) Would the hands of a dear old lady do, Belle? The

A BAD DAY AT GOPHER'S BREATH 53

hands of a sweet little woman who bakes pies every Saturday, who tends to the pigs as if they was her own, who crochets blankets fer ya in the winter . . . ?

BELLE. (*Interrupting.*) Glory be, man! —Who *is* this saint?

RAWHIDE. (*Beaming.*) My mom, Belle. You kin fulfill her lifelong dream!

BAMBI. Oh!! Mom Rawlins *will* have her potato farm in Idaho!!

RAWHIDE. (*Producing a document enthusiastically.*) I already got a down payment on the land. —Wanna see a picture of it? (BAMBI *and* BELLE *eagerly peruse the picture.*)

AMOS. (*Staggering past them toward Downstage Center.*) I see *I* ain't needed no more. (*He falls to his knees.*) —Belle, honey, I'm slippin' fast. I guess I fanned my last pistol, rolled my last bedroll, chawed my last jerky, shot up my last strongbox . . . (*He struggles to his feet, aided by* FAT JACK.)

FAT JACK. Here. Let me help ya, Ol' Hoss . . .

AMOS. (*Beginning to wander Downstage Right, coughing intermittently.*) Thank ya, Fat Jack . . . I done climbed my last mountain, forded my, my last stream, uh, followed my last rainbow . . . , uh, uh . . . (*He's Upstage Right now, struggling against the table; throughout this scene* RABBIT EARS, *sodden on the Upstage Right table, ignores and is ignored by all.*)

BELLE. (*Not overly impressed.*) Save yer strength, Amos

AMOS. No, Belle, some things got to be said . . . —Now, where was I? . . . Yeah . . . , I reckon I stole my last kiss, stole my last gold . . . , toasted my last marshmallow, plugged my last rustler, (*Lurches to the bar, and begins sinking from it.*) plugged my last bystander . . . , plugged my last ol' lady an' puppy-dog . . . (*He sinks to the floor.*)

BELLE. Amos, yer talkin' yerself to death . . .

FAT JACK. An' everybody else too!

54 A BAD DAY AT GOPHER'S BREATH

AMOS. (*Rising with effort.*) Leave me finish! I done rode into my last sunset, Belle . . . (*He staggers to Downstage Center and collapses.*) . . . Promise me somethin', will ya . . . ? (*Pauses.*) See to my horse for me; make sure he gets his full measure of oats at the livery . . . (*He fades out, then rises back to his elbows.*) Ya gotta watch ol' Jake—he'll shortchange ya! . . . An' see that Barkeep gets the six bits I still owe him. I got a little money left from sheriff-in' under my bunk . . . You kin keep the rest, Belle . . . Be sure to plant me high on Boot Hill, Belle . . . (*His voice rises.*) I kin feel myself a'driftin' along with the tumblin' tumbleweed . . . I'm a'headin' fer the last round-up . . . An' one last thing, Belle, honey— (*Long pause.*) Please . . . bury me not on the lone prairie . . .

(*At this juncture, AMOS collapses seemingly for good; all turn away. But, then, after a very short pause, guitar and piano break into "Bury Me Not on the Lone Prairie," and AMOS—die-hard that he is— props himself up to sing the first verse of the song, calling the lines out to the four winds. All the others, surprised of course, turn back to him, and then join in for the second and ensuing verses. Other actors not on Stage may join in during the song for a curtain call. AMOS finally—finally—dies at the end of the song.*)

FINAL CURTAIN

O BURY ME NOT ON THE LONE PRAIRIE

"O bury me not on the lone prairie,"
These words came slowly and mournfully
From the pallid lips of a youth who lay
On his cold damp bed at the close of day.

A BAD DAY AT GOPHER'S BREATH 55

"O bury me not on the lone prairie
Where the wild coyote will howl o'er me,
Where the cold wind weeps and the grasses wave;
No sunbeams rest on a prairie grave."

He has wasted and pined till o'er his brow
Death's shades are slowly gathering now;
He thought of his home with his loved ones nigh,
As the cowboys gathered to see him die.

Again he listened to well known words,
To the wind's soft sigh and the song of birds;
He thought of his home and his native bowers,
Where he loved to roam in his childhood hours.

"I've ever wished that when I died,
My grave might be on the old hillside,
Let there the place of my last rest be—
O bury me not on the lone prairie!

O'er my slumbers a mother's prayer
And a sister's tears will be mingled there;
For 'tis sad to know that the heart-throb's o'er,
And that its fountain will gush no more.

In my dreams I say"—but his voice failed there;
And they gave no heed to his dying prayer;
In a narrow grave six feet by three,
They buried him there on the lone prairie.

May the light winged butterfly pause to rest
O'er him who sleeps on the prairie's crest;
May the Texas rose in the breezes wave
O'er him who sleeps in a prairie's grave.

And the cowboys now as they roam the plain,
(For they marked the spot where his bones have lain)
Fling a handful of roses over his grave,
With a prayer to him who his soul will save.

PROPERTY LIST

The Setting

A BAD DAY AT GOPHER'S BREATH is a farce in thirteen scenes whose action changes alternately between three locations, a saloon and bank, typical of the 1880's, and the hideout of the Rawlins gang. The interiors of all three must be suggested. As many groups will find using a proscenium stage convenient or necessary, it may be advised to set up the saloon and bank side-by-side on the stage, Stage Right and Left, respectively. The gang's hideout may be constructed as a 1x2 structure, situated on a low platform in the audience, preferably to the right of and in front. (Floor plans appear at the end of this script.)

For best economy of space, the piano-player should be placed immediately in front of the Stage on the audience's Left.

The locale for Scene 1 is a richly decorated saloon interior; swinging doors are found one-third of the way Upstage on the Stage Right wall. In the Center, on the Upstage wall is a stairway that leads to an upstairs. The stairway angles toward Stage Right. The bar is placed in front of an angling Stage Left wall (Remember that with two sets on Stage, this wall is approximately in the Center). The wood on the bar, wainscoting, tables, and stairs should be dark and rich-looking—it may be simulated by realistic wallpaper or pressed paper panelling. The remainder of the walls should be papered, perhaps red flocked design in the barroom proper and gold-colored paper in the Upstairs hallway area. Behind the bar is a large mirror over which hangs a set of cow horns; this is flanked on either side by (electric) gaslights and two shelves of bottles. There are three tables with accompanying chairs in the room.

Scene 2 occurs within the hideout of the gang. Since the audience must look into the one-room shack from the outside, it is merely a frame which suggests walls and a roofline. Partial walls and roofing may be placed on the two sides away from the viewer. On the low platform—which may be three 4x8 platforms set next to each other—are two folding

PROPERTY LIST 57

cots (small, camping type), placed on the Down and Upstage edges and a table in the Center with three crates in place of chairs. The place is littered with a saddle, blankets, empty cans and wastepaper, and lighting from spotlights is supplemented by a couple of hanging lanterns, wired electrically. The room is always entered through the Upstage Left end.

Finally, access to the bank interior is gained through a door on an angling wall on Stage Right (actually in the Center and completing a "V" with the wall on which the bar is located); to the Left of the door is a window upon which may be reversed letters reading "First Phingerdoo Savings & Trust." To the Left of the window, on a short Upstage wall stands a large safe—or front of one, black, with gold and silver dials and handles, and the letters spelling "Clutzmeyer" in the Center. Beginning in front of the safe and continuing along the Stage Left wall is a partition of dark wood about three feet high, with a teller's cage in it two-thirds of the way Upstage and a gate to the Left of the cage. Behind the partion, on the Downstage end, is a desk and chair. In front of the partition at the same point, is a wooden bench for customers' convenience. In the Downstage Center area is a writing stand, upon which is placed a pen and inkwell. A painting of a founding father hangs upon the long Stage Left wall; there must be an Offstage entrance on the Downstage end of this wall.

INDIVIDUAL PROPERTIES—Check also character descriptions, which include some props, particularly costume items.

NARRATOR: guitar (carried throughout)
SALOON GIRLS: small handbags with drawstrings that may be twirled (used throughout)
BARKEEP: cloth for wiping glasses (used throughout)
AMOS CRUTCHWAFFLE: pocketwatch (used throughout), badge, coin (Scene 1)
DOC: cloth for cleaning his rifle (Scene 2)
RAWHIDE: plan for robbing the bank (Scene 5), extra notes, stuffed in his shirt (Scene 7), leather pouch on a string (Scene 11), photograph (Scene 13)
SLEEPY: bean can, bean (Scene 5)
BAD BRUCE: cigar (Scene 6)

PROPERTY LIST

EXTRA—in Scene 8: apparatus which makes it look like the cowboy has a back full of arrows

PANDORA CRUTCHWAFFLE: balsa sledgehammer, break-away bottle on Downstage Left table with which to hit Amos (both Scene 10)

TEMPERANCE LADIES: instruments—tambourine, bass drum, coronet; lightweight weapons, as parasols, hats (Scene 10)

BELLE DURHAM: pistol (Scene 10 and Scene 13)

BAMBI PHINGERDOO: water glass (Scene 12)

Finally, blank pistols and blank cartridges will be needed (probably three of them) to simulate a realistic gunfight in the darkness of Scene 12. Blanks may also be chosen for use in all other shooting during the play.

SET PROPERTIES—See also The Setting

Saloon:

3 or 4 small round or square tables and about 12 wooden chairs
large mirror with gilt frame to hang over the bar
gaslights or kerosene lamps (electric) to flank the mirror
shelves and assorted bottles to go on them
spittoons
coat and hat rack
tablecloths
glass beer mugs
shot glasses
break-away whiskey bottle
playing cards

Hideout:

a rectangular table with 2 worn-looking chairs
crates to sit on
2 folding cots
a saddle
assorted empty food cans, boxes, wastepaper
cans of beans
kerosene lanterns (electric) that may be hung
saddle blankets
pencil and paper
"maps" of Gopher's Breath and the bank

PROPERTY LIST

Bank:
wooden waiting bench
wooden writing stand
curtains for both wall and door windows
small desk and chair to go behind teller's cage wall
large painting of bank's founder
fountain pens for cage, desk, and writing stand
ink well
note papers and stage money for various business
hanging institution lamps with large white globes, suspended
    from chains (must work)

COSTUME PLOT

Description of Characters—Includes clothing plot

NARRATOR: Middle-aged and rustic. Throughout the play wears conventional frontier garb—vest, large bandana, cowboy hat, boots and jeans, all badly battered. Carries a guitar and sings and speaks in a twangy, western drawl.

BARKEEP: Broad-shouldered and portly, in his mid-thirties. Sports the usual handlebar mustache, has slicked-back hair. He wears a white shirt with sleeve garters, a red vest, black bowtie and a bartender's apron throughout.

MINOR CHARACTERS: During the first scene and other saloon scenes, the Stage is occupied by numerous cowboys, barflies, and extras, all dressed in various nondescript western outfits—cowboy hats and neckerchiefs, chaps, jeans, boots and guns. Different style and color hats, range coats, vests, etc., can be used on extras in various scenes to provide new characters to replace those frequently shot by the sheriff.

SALOON GIRLS, APRIL, MAY and JUNE. The girls wear matching, gaudy-colored 1880's gowns with sequins, low-cut bodices, and floor-length skirts with flounces. They also wear feather boas, lots of tacky costume jewelry (bracelets and rings), and hairdos with cascades of curls piled on top of their heads. All three should appear to be different in shape, sizes and ages, and spend most of their time on stage consorting with the paying customers.

AMOS CRUTCHWAFFLE: The sheriff is an aging gunfighter with hair-trigger reflexes, graying around the temples, and reputed to be the second fastest gun in the West. He is lean, mean, scarred, and wears a patch over his left eye, his hair long and greased back. Wears a black frock coat, vest, string tie, jangling spurs and two guns slung low. When he speaks, his voice is low, raspy and cold-blooded.

COSTUME PLOT 61

BELLE DURHAM: An aging saloon queen, a few years younger than Arros. She has a hard but striking beauty due both to her attire and to her station as proprietress of the establishment. She wears a velvet, floor-length gown, long dark, flowing hair and an over-abundance of jewelry. An optional change of costume to a white ruffled blouse and dark skirt for Scene 13 may be used.

RALPH "RAWHIDE" RAWLINS: As the protagonist, near-hero, and leader of the gang, Rawhide is ruggedly handsome, in his mid-twenties, of medium height with curly blond hair. His costume should be typically western but must contrast with those of the rest of the Rawlins gang by being less disreputable, cleaner, and perhaps lighter in color.

THE RAWLINS GANG: Notorious though they may be, the gang members—to a man—should be characterized as dirty and trailworn, basically ignorant, and painfully inept. Individually, they are:

BAD BRUCE: The coarsest and grubbiest of a coarse and grubby lot. A large, raw-boned, bewhiskered and dirty outlaw. He is horribly dense and slow to comprehend. He should wear badly worn, very dirty and dusty, dark-colored western clothing. During the robbery scene (12), Bruce wears a long dark coat and clerical collar of a preacher; the rest of his costume remains the same.

RINGO and LAREDO: Taken together, they are more nondescript gang members with less obvious characteristics than the others, although general tendencies still will apply (ineptitude, etc.). Costumes should reflect their "down-on-their-luck" outlaw status, and in Scene 12, will both wear the obvious bad disguise of a woman's dress over the rest of their outfits. Even in disguise, however, they retain hats, guns, boots, etc., visibly.

DOC: A classic gunfighter type; cold, calculating and mean. A loner particularly antagonistic to Bruce, he is a notch above the others in intelligence. He dresses in an all-black, tight-fitting outfit (flat-crowned gambler's hat, ringed with conches, a vest and knee-high boots.) He carries a rifle at all times and disdains wearing a disguise in Scene 12.

COSTUME PLOT

SLEEPY: Conventional costume like Ringo and Laredo. A submissive, spineless and gullible character, he is a born follower. Wears a more complete woman's outfit in Scene 12, including a hat and handbag.

DOPEY: Tall and gangling, his costume should be several sizes too small. The epitome of everything wrong with the Rawlins gang, he is the stupidest, clumsiest, most unaware bandit of the lot.

BAMBI PHINGERDOO: Bambi is young, beautiful, and rosy-cheeked, and above all else, naive and innocent. When she appears in Scene 3, the heroine wears a modest floor-length gingham dress. Scenes 7 and 12 require costume changes to dresses similar to Bambi's first outfit, also light and cheerful; prints perhaps.

COGGINS, THE BANK TELLER: Old, decrepit, and hard of hearing. He wears dark trousers, a white shirt and string tie of the period; also rimless glasses and a green eyeshade visor.

GENERAL CUSTER: The famed commander of the 7th. should have shoulder-length blond hair or wig, a fringed buckskin jacket, striped military trousers, and sword. Beneath his jacket protrude the holsters of twin pearl-handled silver revolvers. Of course, he is mustachioed with a goatee. He wears a cavalry cap.

RABBIT EARS, THE DRUNKEN INDIAN: Dark and swarthy. Also, long black hair drawn back into braids, dirty moth-eaten buckskins and moccasins, black felt Navaho hat with two broken feathers stuck in the brim, one above each ear. Traces of faded war-paint.

PANDORA CRUTCHWAFFLE: A very large, buxom woman, bulging with propriety. In her late fifties, she wears her graying hair pulled back into a tight bun; her costume is severe, a plain dark dress with imposing bustle. She also wears high-buttoned shoes, a small unobtrusive hat, and carries a weapon (a balsa wood sledgehammer is preferred).

COSTUME PLOT

OTHER TEMPERANCE LADIES: All should be dressed in costumes similar to Pandora's, proper, middle-aged, middle-class attire of the period. They should stay with muted colors, a hat or two of more flambuoyant color is permissible. They should all be smaller in size than Pandora, and should act in unison, following the orchestrations of their leader. They carry musical instruments and instruments of destruction.

FAT JACK CALDWELL: Fat Jack is the antithesis of what everyone expects. He is pencil-thin, blond, mustachioed, and pale. He wears white fringed buckskins, white furry chaps, and red-white-and-blue boots. His hat and twin pistols, also color-coordinated—are far too small, almost child-like. He speaks with a high, thin voice.

PIANO-PLAYER: This part is optional, as the piano—used between scenes and during the opening of Scene 10—may remain Offstage. If played out front and by a male, he would wear a pin-striped shirt with added collar, dark trousers, sleeve bands, and probably a mustache. If a girl is your pianist, she should wear a white blouse and long skirt.

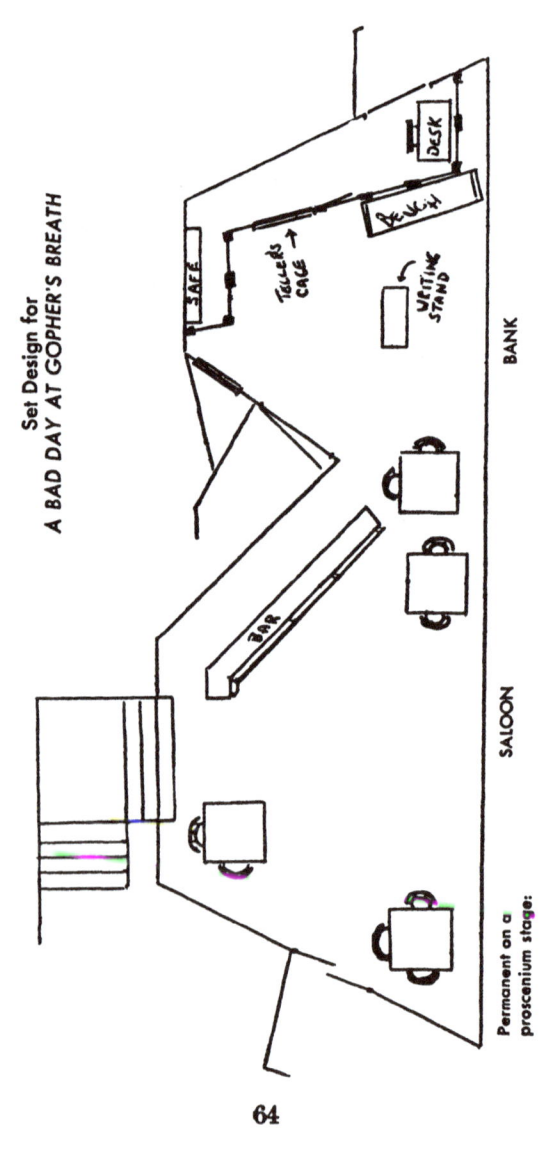

THE SCENE
Theresa Rebeck

Little Theatre / Drama / 2m, 2f / Interior Unit Set
A young social climber leads an actor into an extra-marital affair, from which he then creates a full-on downward spiral into alcoholism and bummery. His wife runs off with his best friend, his girlfriend leaves, and he's left with… nothing.

"Ms. Rebeck's dark-hued morality tale contains enough fresh insights into the cultural landscape to freshen what is essentially a classic boy-meets-bad-girl story."
- *New York Times*

"Rebeck's wickedly scathing observations about the sort of self-obsessed New Yorkers who pursue their own interests at the cost of their morality and loyalty."
- *New York Post*

"The Scene is utterly delightful in its comedic performances, and its slowly unraveling plot is thought-provoking and gut-wrenching."
- *Show Business Weekly*

THREE MUSKETEERS
Ken Ludwig

All Groups / Adventure / 8m, 4f (doubling) / Unit sets
This adaptation is based on the timeless swashbuckler by Alexandre Dumas, a tale of heroism, treachery, close escapes and above all, honor. The story, set in 1625, begins with d'Artagnan who sets off for Paris in search of adventure. Along with d'Artagnan goes Sabine, his sister, the quintessential tomboy. Sent with d'Artagnan to attend a convent school in Paris, she poses as a young man – d'Artagnan's servant – and quickly becomes entangled in her brother's adventures. Soon after reaching Paris, d'Artagnan encounters the greatest heroes of the day, Athos, Porthos and Aramis, the famous musketeers; d'Artagnan joins forces with his heroes to defend the honor of the Queen of France. In so doing, he finds himself in opposition to the most dangerous man in Europe, Cardinal Richelieu. Even more deadly is the infamous Countess de Winter, known as Milady, who will stop at nothing to revenge herself on d'Artagnan – and Sabine – for their meddlesome behavior. Little does Milady know that the young girl she scorns, Sabine, will ultimately save the day.

THE MUSICAL OF MUSICALS (THE MUSICAL!)
Music by Eric Rockwell
Lyrics by Joanne Bogart
Book by Eric Rockwell and Joanne Bogart

2m, 2f / Musical / Unit Set

The Musical of Musicals (The Musical!) is a musical about musicals! In this hilarious satire of musical theatre, one story becomes five delightful musicals, each written in the distinctive style of a different master of the form, from Rodgers and Hammerstein to Stephen Sondheim. The basic plot: June is an ingenue who can't pay the rent and is threatened by her evil landlord. Will the handsome leading man come to the rescue? The variations are: a Rodgers & Hammerstein version, set in Kansas in August, complete with a dream ballet; a Sondheim version, featuring the landlord as a tortured artistic genius who slashes the throats of his tenants in revenge for not appreciating his work; a Jerry Herman version, as a splashy star vehicle; an Andrew Lloyd Webber version, a rock musical with themes borrowed from Puccini; and a Kander & Ebb version, set in a speakeasy in Chicago. This comic valentine to musical theatre was the longest running show in the York Theatre Company's 35-year history before moving to Off-Broadway.

"Witty! Refreshing! Juicily! Merciless!"
- Michael Feingold, *Village Voice*

"A GIFT FROM THE MUSICAL THEATRE GODS!"
– *TalkinBroadway.com*

"Real Wit, Real Charm! Two Smart Writers and Four Winning Performers! You get the picture, it's GREAT FUN!"
- *The New York Times*

"Funny, charming and refreshing!
It hits its targets with sophisticated affection!"
- *New York Magazine*

SAMUELFRENCH.COM

www.ingramcontent.com/pod-product-compliance
Lightning Source LLC
Chambersburg PA
CBHW070649300426
44111CB00013B/2343